# POSITIONED TO BLESS

## ALSO BY FAISAL MALICK

*The Destiny of Islam in the End Times*

AVAILABLE FROM DESTINY IMAGE PUBLISHERS

# POSITIONED TO BLESS

Secrets to Fulfilling Your Divine Assignment

FAISAL MALICK

capitalized. We choose not to acknowledge him, even to the point of violating grammatical rules.

**DESTINY IMAGE® PUBLISHERS, INC.**
**P.O. Box 310, Shippensburg, PA 17257-0310**

*"Speaking to the Purposes of God for this Generation and for the Generations to Come."*

This book and all other Destiny Image, Revival Press, Mercy Place, Fresh Bread, Destiny Image Fiction, and Treasure House books are available at Christian bookstores and distributors worldwide.

For a U.S. bookstore nearest you, call 1-800-722-6774.

For more information on foreign distributors, call 717-532-3040.

Reach us on the Internet: www.destinyimage.com.

ISBN 10: 0-7684-2694-4
ISBN 13: 978-0-7684-2694-6

For Worldwide Distribution, Printed in the U.S.A.

1 2 3 4 5 6 7 8 9 10 11 / 12 11 10 09 08

# DEDICATION

I dedicate this book to the millions who live in the shadows but are called to live in the light. To those of you who have walked in the wilderness, far too long, and not yet tasted of the Promised Land. To those considered not so wise and not so noble in the eyes of man yet part of the divine tapestry and blueprint for this new era. To all who've been alone without a people, place, or country to call your own. To you who were sent into battle without weapons and left discouraged and to all who've been rejected because your time was not yet come.

It is your season to be divinely positioned into your place of authority under the Sovereign Hand of the Lord, leaving your enemies powerless. In the midst of shifts and shakings, God is aligning your life to precede a season of divine assignment that carries eternal significance on earth.

God has heard the cry of your heart. He has come to raise you up out of the ashes and reposition you into your place of divine destiny.

I believe that as you read through the pages of this book you will come to a revelation that what man has tolerated about your differences, God will celebrate in this season. You will start living a passionate life fueled by purpose and positioned to leave a legacy that will transform the generations to come. You will dare to live a life of eternal significance.

Have you ever thought something or someone is opposing your destiny? You're right. Are you stuck in the same place you were five years ago? Faisal Malick uncovers ancient Kingdom strategies to get you to your assignment. This book is a Holy Spirit GPS to destiny!

Sid Roth

Television host, "It's Supernatural!"

Do you want to effectively influence others with the Father's love, integrity, and truth? Do you desire to finish your course strong? If so, this book is for you. Faisal Malick shares important insights and revelations for the development of mature, faithful believers in Christ. *Positioned to Bless* invites you to engage in a valuable journey that will posture you to be blessed and to bless.

Patricia King

www.xpmedia.com

Faisal Malick has a unique perspective on the Body of Christ. As a Muslim who was called by Christ and answered the call, he has experienced spiritual warfare and the power of Christ in ways many of us have never known. He shares this perspective with us in his new book, *Positioned to Bless*. He unveils the secrets of overcoming every test and trial that life presents in order to reach the authority and position God has intended for us. Faisal's book is instructive as well as prophetic. His ministry is fueled by the love of God.

DR. RON BURGIO
President, Elim Fellowship, Lima, New York
Senior Pastor, Love Joy Gospel Church,
Lancaster, New York

# CONTENTS

*For You created my inmost being;*
*You knit me together in my mother's womb.*
*I praise You because I am fearfully*
*and wonderfully made;*
*Your works are wonderful,*
*I know that full well.*
*My frame was not hidden from You*
*when I was made in the secret place.*
*When I was woven together in the*
*depths of the earth,*
*Your eyes saw my unformed body.*
*All the days ordained for me*
*were written in Your book*
*before one of them came to be.*
(Psalm 139:13-16 NIV)

# INTRODUCTION

*Before I formed you in the womb*
*I knew you;*
*before you were born I sanctified you;*
*I ordained you a prophet to the nations*
(Jeremiah 1:5).

Have you ever had a cry in your heart—a desire from God to see certain things come to pass—but year after year nothing seems to happen? Have you ever felt destined for greater things, but remain feeling stuck in a powerless place? Has it ever appeared as though what God said to you was about to happen when suddenly it was swept away from your grasp?

It might not seem like it now, but you are being strategically positioned in the spirit. You may move from one place to the next geographically, or you may live in the same small town all of your life; but that will not affect the authority God has given you to impact this world. God has prepared a strategic location—or region—for you individually, and others God connects you with corporately, to reign over in the spirit. If you will hear His voice, He will bring you out of any dark place you find yourself and empower you to take the throne of influence He has designated for you. When you take your seat of authority in the Kingdom, you will be operating from a place of divine favor and blessing enabling you to win eternal victories for Christ. You will be positioned to fulfill your unique Kingdom assignment.

Next to your relationship with the Father, Son and Holy Spirit, there is nothing more important than for you to understand and accept your place of authority in the Kingdom. There is more to being a Christian than getting saved. There is more to living in the Kingdom of Light than obtaining an address on Glory Street and setting up a comfortable house. You have an assignment. For you to grow up and mature in Christ, you must learn to step into the place of authority God has prepared for you so you can fulfill the assignment you were created for.

If you are like most believers, you sense there is something more to your life than what you've experienced so far—you have an inner conviction that there is a greater purpose and eternal significance to your presence on this planet. And you are right. There is a divine assignment that the Lord has designated for you alone.

It is my hope that by the time you finish reading this book, you will be in a position to step into your strategic place of authority—you will be able to confidently sit in the seat of authority God has prepared to propel you to your destiny. You will learn to posture yourself correctly and accurately. You will be perfectly positioned for the very thing that is divinely unique and eternal about your life.

By the time you finish reading this strategic manual—what I'm calling a "GPS to destiny"—you will be equipped to overcome every enemy that opposes you, to pass every test that is preparing you, and to walk in the authority God has ordained for you. You will learn David's tactics for conquering giants, surviving the wilderness, and leading great armies to victory. Like David, you will learn to forge powerful alliances, and in so doing, unleash the massive potential hidden within you and those in your sphere of influence. I will show you how to navigate this extraordinary Kingdom responsibility and how to embrace the supernatural weight of authority that will rest upon you as a result.

The earth is undergoing a major shift, a season of dramatic change. There is a new move of the Spirit involving vast transfers of power. God is repositioning His people in all spheres of leadership. He is in the process of replacing certain positions that have been held by unholy forces with His own instruments of righteous authority—vessels created for honor and influence such as you and I. When that transfer takes place, there will be a dramatic shift in the power structure and a noticeable change in the atmosphere.

These are exciting, as well as demanding, times. God is unfolding unprecedented wonders on a global scale, but He is also calling upon each one of His followers to rise up in the power and authority He has ordained for them. Now is the time. God is calling you to step forward, to rise up, and to sit down in the seat of authority He has prepared for you.

Just as Christ Jesus rose up to take His seat at the right hand of the Father, the Body of Christ—His Church—is being called to rise up and take her seat of authority in the earth. You are an integral part of that Body; each and every one of you is designed and destined to sit in a particular seat of authority that has been prepared for you alone since the dawn of time. Without every member seated in his or her proper place, operating in his or her full authority, the Body as a whole will continue to be impotent and powerless.

I pray that as you read this God will reveal to your heart those mysteries concerning you, your house, and your ministry—and that the Holy Spirit awakens your mind to the invaluable anointing on your life. May this book help you to confidently step into your place of authority and firmly establish you in your calling. May you rise up to take your seat and more deliberately and powerfully fulfill your divine assignment. For you have been called for such a time as this.

# CHAPTER 1

# THE SECRET OF THE SEAT

*And I heard every creature in heaven*
*and on earth*
*and under the earth and in the sea, and*
*all that is in them, saying,*
*"To Him who sits on the throne*
*and to the Lamb*
*be blessing and honor and glory and*
*might forever and ever!"*
(Revelation 5:13 ESV)

We are on the threshold of a new era. A culmination of the ages is coming upon the Church. There is a door that is being closed behind us and a new door that is being opened before us. The Spirit of God wants us to walk as a people through this new door and step into a realm that we've never walked in or experienced before. It is a realm of power. More specifically, it is the realm of God's divine authority—of God's eternal purposes coming to pass. It is a realm where you will see God do what you have never before dreamed or imagined.

The eternal purposes that you are called to be a part of are wrapped in a season—in a particular moment of time. Your divine assignment is wrapped in a *kairos* moment, when God begins to say, "Now is the time!" *Kairos* is a Greek word meaning "a God-appointed moment or season"—a defining moment when all things come together to change the course of human history. There is an appointed time for Kingdom advancement across this threshold. The minute we cross this threshold as a Body, as a Church, we will see the Kingdom advance like it has never advanced in 2,000 years of church history. This is the era that is upon us.

So what do I hear the Lord saying to you? *"Be prepared!"*

I hear the Lord saying, *"Get ready!"*

You have been in a season of preparation. This has been a season of alignment. God is aligning people. He is sifting and shifting His people. The Lord is causing His people to make changes, to look deep into their hearts, and to consecrate their lives. As Joshua 3:5

(NIV) says, *"Consecrate yourselves, for tomorrow the Lord will do amazing things among you."* This is the era when God will do amazing things among us. But once we cross over this threshold, there is no turning back.

## CROSSING OVER

*Are You not the One who dried up the sea,*
*the waters of the great deep; that made the*
*depths of the sea a road for the redeemed*
*to cross over?* (Isaiah 51:10)

God has begun positioning the Church. He is preparing the Body of Christ to cross over into a new era. There is a radical shift occurring in the Church throughout the world. There is a line being drawn that we are going to cross over—as a Church and as individuals—and as we do, entire regions will follow. If there was ever a question in your mind about what you were uniquely designed or engineered for, it will become clear. When you step over

> *When you step over into the arena God has called you to, the unique expression of the Father in Christ that is hidden within you will begin to come forth.*

into the arena God has called you to, the unique expression of the Father in Christ that is hidden within you will begin to come forth. It is my prayer that as you read this, the Holy Spirit will begin to speak to you regarding the treasure God has placed within you.

Some of you are not yet fully aware of the treasure you possess—the gift you were created to be to the world. But now is the time when God will begin to speak to the treasure that is hidden within you. He will begin calling it forth without measure as this new door opens upon us. As those treasures hidden in your heart are more clearly revealed, your divine assignment will become increasingly evident.

What do I mean by your divine assignment? Your divine assignment is the eternal purpose for which you were created; it is what you were put on this earth to complete. It is the foreordained purpose God had in mind for you before you were even born. It is what you were set apart and ordained to do in your life. When one of us steps into our individual assignment, there is a tremendous impact for the Kingdom. Imagine what would happen if 100, or 1,000, or 100,000 of us stepped into our divine assignment. The Church of the Lord Jesus Christ as a body would move corporately forward advancing the Kingdom like never before in history.

This is such a time. God has been speaking to me

about the shift that is taking place in this season—how He is repositioning His people and bringing alignment to His Church. God has a corporate eternal purpose involving every individual in the Body of Christ in this era—in this *kairos* season in the earth. He needs every single person in the Body to be positioned in their assignment to propel the Kingdom forward like never before.

**THIS IS THE SEASON WE ARE STEPPING INTO!**

The Lord is positioning people in places of unprecedented authority. We are entering an age of the government of God on the earth such as history has never before witnessed. Not only will we see the gifts of God in operation in what were once the darkest recesses of the planet, but we will also see the government of the Kingdom of God operating at the very highest levels of power. A governmental authority is going to come upon the Church—a governmental authority that will displace all authorities that are not of God.

Major shifts in every sphere of influence will propel the people of God into places of power throughout the earth. These are bold statements, but the hour is upon us for the Bride to take her place at the wedding table. A place has been prepared for her, and when she takes her seat, a new order will be established.

I am not giving you information here; I am imparting revelation—things that can only be spiritually discerned. Revelation is the life of God written upon your hearts. Information, or knowledge, is the illumination of the life written upon your spirit that goes into your mind so you can grasp how the Spirit of God is moving.

God wants to give you a revelation. You will see that where there is revelation, there is also a divine impartation. You will notice that when this impartation begins to take place, the treasure hidden within you will begin to come forth. Pray this with me now:

> *Father,*
> *I submit to Your divine authority. I thank You for Your Spirit; I thank You for revelation knowledge. Thank You for Your eternal purpose and the call and the assignment that is on my life. I submit my life to You, I lay down my personal agenda, I lay down my own vision, and I will catch Your vision. I will obey. Please show me Your ways; teach me how to walk in Your ways. Help me to know You and to understand the holy call You've placed upon me. Give me strength. Enlarge my capacity to withstand more of Your glory, more of Your presence. Enlarge my capacity to walk in Your ways.*

*Make me a container larger than ever before in the spirit so I can receive revelation knowledge. Train me, Lord; make me skillful in the word of righteousness so that in the time of battle I can successfully wield the sword of the Spirit in Jesus' mighty name. Amen.*

## COME OUT OF THE CAVE

[David] *has... hidden in some pit or cave. And when he comes out and attacks... there will be panic among your troops...* (2 Samuel 17:9 NLT).

I have seen many people with great callings upon their lives. Sometimes, however, it seems as if the greater the calling, the more confined they are—the more locked up they are, so to speak. I prophetically began to see that there are many people like David who have a call of God—who are anointed, gifted, and have a heart after God—but are stuck in a cave hiding from the enemy. I began to see these people in the Church, and as I looked across the Body of Christ, the Lord spoke to me, saying, "It's time for My Davids to come out of their caves."

Now I understand what it is like to be stuck in a cave. I am intimately familiar with what happens in the dark recesses of a spiritual cave—and the mindset that results from the negative conditioning that takes place. Sometimes fear can keep you in a cave, or a place of rejection or opposition. Sometimes God can put you there for a season as a place of sanctuary. But it is time to come out! I began to see that although many people are anointed and gifted in their area of assignment, they are held captive by a cave mentality. This mindset keeps them from stepping out into the realm of authority that will position them to fulfill their assignment.

> *I began to see that although many people are anointed and gifted in their area of assignment, they are held captive by a cave mentality.*

I began to see people like Joseph, who from a young age have had a heart and vision for what God is calling them to do. These people are struggling to obey God, yet they find themselves stuck in a prison. People like Joseph are called and anointed; yet they have no place—no position—from which they can fulfill their assignment. I began to see that there are people today who are not fulfilling what God is calling them to do because they are unable to step into the place of authority God has prepared for them. Although the enemy is defeated and the prison doors are wide open, many people remain in the cell, held captive by their own shame, doubt, or fear.

I have learned that you can be called, gifted, and anointed—you can have a heart after God—but if you are not positioned in your proper seat of authority you will never be able to fulfill your assignment. If you don't take your seat in the place of authority God has prepared for you, you will never fulfill the vision that God has placed in your heart. God

> *If you don't take your seat in the place of authority God has prepared for you, you will never fulfill the vision that God has placed in your heart.*

began to show me how it is that the Spirit of God positions people. He began to reveal how we are to step into our assigned seats of authority in order to fulfill our divine assignments.

Whatever your sphere is, once you step into your seat of authority, you will begin to influence what it is that God has called you to affect. The enemy will do anything to keep you from sitting in your seat, because once you sit in your seat, his ability to oppose you changes. The enemy knows that once you take your seat in this God-ordained place of authority, what you decree becomes law.

Your seat represents a divine order that is backed by Heaven itself. When you are in your seat, a corporate hand comes upon you because your seat is not about you; it is about God's eternal purpose and the assignment He has entrusted to you. The assignment God has for you is located in your place of authority. Most people never fulfill their assignment because they never sit in their seat of authority.

Most Christians are faithful to attend church, worship, pray, and serve. God loves those things—they touch His heart. But one day, He wants you to sit in the seat you were destined to sit in so that you can fulfill the assignment He has for you in this lifetime. He wants you to learn to exercise your authority and take dominion over the things He has placed in your care.

## A PLACE OF POWER AND SAFETY

*But when you cross over...and dwell in the land which the Lord your God is giving you to inherit...He gives you rest from all your enemies round about, so that you dwell in safety* (Deuteronomy 12:10).

All of this time you have been growing and maturing and becoming more gifted. "God," you say, "I've heard every prophecy. I've heard every '*word of the Lord*.' I've tried to do all You have told me to, yet I still haven't touched my purpose! I still haven't hit the significance of my life." You may experience a few signs and wonders—a sprinkling of God's power—so then you declare, "God, I separate myself to the work You have called me to"—and next you find yourself in a testing season.

Here in the wilderness, as you get closer to God, a stronger power comes on you. You are able to say; "Now I can do it! Perhaps this is my chance!" You try to do great things for the Lord, but fall short. You convince yourself that you never really felt God's power; or perhaps you did but the enemy promptly knocked the wind out of you; or you stumbled and decided you were never worthy. But in truth, you simply missed the purpose behind God's empowering.

The power of God comes upon you to get you to your seat. The enemy whom you thought was trying to keep you from your assignment was actually trying to keep you from your seat—because as long as he can keep you from your seat, he can keep you from fulfilling your assignment.

> *The power of God comes upon you to get you to your seat.*

The highest place of authority in the Kingdom is to be seated in the place God has called you to sit. Once you are in your seat, it is all over between you and the enemy.

Once you are positioned in your seat of authority, you are seated in God's authority, and nothing can successfully oppose you there. This is the secret place of the Most High! Sure, the enemy will hit you with his best shot, but when you are in that place under the hand of God, *"No weapon formed against you shall prosper"* (Isa. 54:17).

In Acts chapter 13, we read about the Holy Spirit launching Paul and Barnabas into their divine assignment. The Holy Spirit sent them off, but more than that, He positioned them in their seat of authority. We know this because of what happens a little farther down in the chapter. When Paul goes to speak to a governor, a sorcerer attempts to interfere. We read in Acts 13:10-11 that Paul says, *"You son of the devil, you enemy of all righteousness, will you not cease perverting the straight ways of the Lord? And now...you shall be blind, not seeing the sun for a time."* And the man goes blind! Now how often have you had the authority to strike someone blind? Paul had the authority because he was sitting in his seat. Anything that came against him met with the hand of the Lord.

> *Your seat of authority is intricately connected to your eternal purpose, or the divine assignment upon your life.*

Your seat of authority is intricately connected to your

eternal purpose, or the divine assignment upon your life. Do you remember Elijah? Do you remember how the hand of the Lord came upon him and he outran the king's chariots? The hand of the Lord came upon him because he was occupying his seat of authority. Elijah fulfilled his assignment because he was seated in the place of authority God had designed for him. In Ezekiel 8:1 we read, *"And it came to pass in the sixth year, in the sixth month, on the fifth day of the month"*—in other words, in the appointed time—*"as I sat in my house with the elders of Judah sitting before me, that the hand of the Lord God fell upon me there."* Whenever you sit in your seat the hand of the Lord will come upon you.

Now prior to this, in Ezekiel 3:22, we read, "The hand of the Lord was upon me there, and He said to me, 'Arise, go out into the plain, and there I shall talk with you.'" The Hebrew word for *arise* that is used here means "get yourself to a higher level." God is essentially telling Ezekiel, "Arise, go forth to a higher plane." Ezekiel arose and went forth, and the glory of the Lord came and stood before him. God spoke to him. Have you ever heard God telling you, "Come up higher, come up higher…. You're doing really well; could you come up higher and take your seat?"

Of course as a Christian, you are seated in Christ. From this position you are able to practice a certain authority over your own circumstances in Jesus' name.

You can pray with authority over your individual situation. In the family, it is easy to understand the authority that parents have over their children. A husband has authority to bring a blessing to his spouse and family. Each of you has a certain jurisdiction of authority in your own home. But I can't come to your home and have that same authority, is that right?

As the spiritual heads of our homes, God uses us to be a blessing to our family. But when we talk about exercising authority regarding our divine assignment, this is where people usually miss it. They try to deal with the enemy from the standpoint of their individual authority—authority they have been granted over their family, property, or personal circumstances. They are attempting to exercise a personal-level authority over a corporate-level enemy of God.

So what is a corporate enemy? A corporate enemy is the enemy that is opposing God's eternal purposes—not people like you and I. On the other hand, there is an individual enemy who does oppose individual believers. We have all come up against some devils, have we not? We've slaughtered a few, haven't we? God gave us the authority to come against any demon that dares intrude on our property or in our personal lives in any way.

But sometimes we are dealing with an enemy that, let's be honest, we don't feel like we're winning against.

That type of enemy is not an individual enemy. That is a corporate enemy that is opposing the eternal purposes of God and therefore the divine assignment on your life. You cannot deal with that devil the same way you deal with those pesky personal devils. These extra crispy devils need to be dealt with by the hand of the Lord. So the key is not to engage those crispier devils in hand-to-hand combat, but to quickly get over to your seat and let the Lord flick them away.

The enemy is trying to draw you into the ring when all you need to do is get to your seat. That should be your only focus. Like in musical chairs, once you make it into your seat you're safe. You run for that seat as fast you can. How do you do that? You determine to obey God no matter what comes at you. You say, "I'm not going to let the devil trip me up; I'm not going to let the devil distract me; I'm going to do what I need to do. I'm going to make it over to that seat!" Then you sit down in your seat of authority, and when that corporate devil comes against you, he'll come up against the hand of the Lord! If you are firmly planted in your seat, the hand of the Lord is firmly

*If you are firmly planted in your seat, the hand of the Lord is firmly planted on you—and that is a very safe place to be.*

planted on you—and that is a very safe place to be.

## VISION VERSUS DESTINY

*Yet who knows whether you have come to the kingdom for such a time as this?* (Esther 4:14)

Although your assignment is personal, it's not about you. Even though God has called you to a special place, a place He has prepared just for you—*for such a time as this*—that one-of-a-kind, custom-designed vision God has placed on your heart is not actually about you at all. Your individual assignment is about God's eternal purpose on earth. It has to do with the eons of history that have come before you and all of the generations that will follow.

So what is the significance of your personal vision? In Proverbs 29:18 (KJV) we read, *"Where there is no vision, the people perish."* We translate that to mean, "People without vision perish." Does that mean you and I will perish without a vision? What does the word *vision* in this verse of Scripture actually mean? Is it talking about any vision? Hitler had a vision and many people perished! So what kind of vision is the Scripture referring to here?

The word *vision* used in Proverbs 29:18 is specifically referring to "a prophetic revelation." In other words, what is revealed when you look into the eternal purposes of God in relation to the divine assignment He has prepared for you individually, as well as corporately? This is what the writer of Hebrews was referring to in Hebrews 12:2, *"Looking unto Jesus, the author and finisher of our faith, who for the joy that was set before Him endured the cross, despising the shame, and has sat down at the right hand of the throne of God."* Jesus was looking at God's revealed purpose—or vision—for His life on earth.

Jesus understood His role—or His assignment—within the greater context of God's eternal purpose. In this verse, when the author refers to *"the joy that was set before Him,"* he is talking about the *vision* set before Christ. Jesus endured the shame of the cross because He had a prophetic revelation of His divine assignment within the eternal purpose of God. Jesus understood the seat of authority He would need to occupy in order to complete His earthly assignment. As a result, He was promoted to a higher seat from where He now performs His eternal, heavenly ministry. He is the mediator of the New Covenant—our High Priest who is forever interceding on our behalf. He is also our advocate before the Father and head over His Body, the Church.

For every assignment there is a seat of authority. Jesus fulfilled His assignment, and God promoted Him to a seat at His right hand. God has also prepared a heavenly seat for you and me. When we fulfill our assignment here, we will have something else waiting for us in eternity. God is a God of promotion. Think about Joseph from the Old Testament. He had a vision—a prophetic revelation of the heart of God while he was a mere shepherd boy. So why would God show this young sheep herder a vision of something he was not in a position to understand, let alone fulfill? Because Joseph's vision was not about him; it was about God's eternal plan for humanity.

When Joseph shared this prophetic revelation with his brothers, they threw him into a pit. But instead of killing him, they sold him into slavery. He was taken to the land of Egypt where he was sold into his destiny. In order for Joseph to fulfill his divine assignment, he needed to be repositioned. God was fulfilling His Word to Abraham. Regardless of what he wanted or understood, Joseph was headed for the seat of authority in Pharaoh's palace. Joseph was on assignment. And although he was faithful and obedient—although he never "missed it"—he could not bypass the depths of

> *Although he* [Joseph] *was faithful and obedient—although he never "missed it"—he could not bypass the depths of the pit, the bondage of slavery, or the years in prison.*

the pit, the bondage of slavery, or the years in prison. They were all part of his preparation.

Yet even while Joseph was in prison, God's hand was upon him. He experienced divine favor in every place he found himself. When the appointed time for Joseph to step into his seat arrived, he was in position. He was ready. In the span of one day, Joseph was called out of prison and became the second-most powerful person in the world. Joseph took his place at the right hand of Pharaoh, but still, after all he had been through, his promotion was not about his own redemption. Joseph was now positioned to save his nation and to bring the seed of Abraham into Egypt so God could fulfill His promise to Abraham. (See Genesis 15.) Joseph was working out an eternal purpose bigger than his own individual destiny.

## IN LIGHT OF ETERNITY

*I have seen the burden God has placed on us all. Yet God has made everything beautiful for its own time. He has planted eternity in the human heart, but even so, people cannot see the whole scope of God's work from beginning to end (Ecclesiastes 3:10-11 NLT).*

Joseph's destiny was much greater than God's purpose for him personally. God chose Joseph for a divine purpose that was connected from eternity past all the way forward to the end of time. That is how God sees your life—connected with all of eternity. This is what God had in mind when He designated His divine assignment to you—His eternal purpose for your life. He is always thinking from a foreordained perspective based on the book He wrote about you before you were formed and came to exist in the flesh. God is working out your foreordained purpose in conjunction with the divine assignments of others who have come before and will come after you. This is what we see played out in the life of Joseph.

When God made His initial covenant with Abraham, He caused him to fall into a deep sleep. He showed him a future concerning his seed that would not come until generations later when they would find themselves in a foreign, hostile land. God had already written a book on Moses and Joseph and Pharaoh and Abraham with all of this in mind. He also destined for all of these men to have free will, yet God in His sovereignty divinely influenced their hearts to respond to His purpose (without violating their ability to choose). Through the struggles that took place deep within each of their hearts, God fulfilled the eternal purpose He revealed in the promise He made to

Abraham in Genesis 12:3: *"In you all the families of the earth shall be blessed."* That blessing was made manifest in Jesus, the *"Lamb slain from the foundation of the world"* (Rev. 13:8).

Can you imagine seeing your life and purpose on earth through the eternal mind of God? Can you imagine how differently you might fight your battles if you understood God's corporate purpose for your existence? It takes a leap of faith to see your life like God sees it. If you realized you were created for a unique assignment that required you to learn His ways and walk in them, you would find new strength in the midst of your cave experience and resolve to be more single-minded about making it to your throne. If you could see the anticipation with which all of creation waits for you to take your seat of authority, you would walk with a much greater degree of intention and expectancy.

> *If you could see the anticipation with which all of creation waits for you to take your seat of authority, you would walk with a much greater degree of intention and expectancy.*

Abraham did not know God was going to raise up Pharaoh above any other king in the earth and then use his throne to introduce Himself as the God of Israel through his descendant Joseph. Joseph did not know he would come alongside that king to show forth God's faithfulness to what would become the 12 tribes of Israel, as well as forever change the course of two nations. Joseph only began to understand his true purpose when he got into his seat. From that point on he spent the rest of his life walking out a divine assignment that went beyond his personal destiny; it was a corporate destiny that he walked out on behalf of all humanity.

The same can be said of Moses, David, Daniel, Esther, Mary, Peter, and Paul; and the list goes on and on and has not yet come to an end. I believe the time we are moving into will prove to mankind the truth spoken of in Daniel 4:17: *"That the Most High rules in the kingdom of men, gives it to whomever He will, and sets over it the lowest of men."*

Your divine assignment is always part of a greater assignment in the Kingdom. Whether it seems like it or not, your personal vision is interconnected to all of the Kingdom purposes at work in the Body of Christ. There is a regional, national, and global assignment that God is bringing to pass through you. And like Joseph, when you rise up to take your seat in the larger plan, when you see the impact you are having on history and in your nation, you won't regret the dark night in the pit or the years spent in prison.

If you are like me, at some point you have asked yourself, "What is the point of those dark days and nights? Why would God want the children of Israel to end up in Egypt in the first place?" We know that God told Abraham that one day He would bring them out. But why did God send them into bondage just to bring them out again? Why would God want His children to suffer 400 years of slavery before sending Moses to deliver them? And then, when they are finally liberated, why would God lead them straight into the wilderness to wander in circles for 40 years?

There are multiple levels to God's eternal purposes. On the one hand, He positioned Pharaoh as the most powerful man in all the earth. Then God hardened his heart for the purpose of demonstrating that His power was far above that of any king, god, or priest. The whole world would know the God of Israel. But that was not all; He demonstrated His ability to position His servants, and His willingness to work through ordinary men—such as Joseph and Moses—to accomplish extraordinary things.

But what else was God doing? He was giving us a blueprint that would enable us to see the power in the blood of Jesus. He showed us the message of the Passover: Judgment passed over all who came under the blood of the Passover lamb in the same way it passes over those of us who are hidden in Christ. (See Exodus 12.)

God had to have a Passover so one day Jesus could be the fulfillment of it—so you and I could come out of the symbolic bondage of Egypt and enter into the freedom of being in Christ.

There was a far-reaching assignment on Joseph's life. The Church is about to step into this type of generational and governmental assignment. God is beginning to realign the Church and reposition His people. The Lord will begin to deal with your personal life, with your vision, your relationships, and your finances. You may experience opposition like never before. But much of the opposition in your life is not about you; it's about your assignment.

*The key to your assignment can be found in the opposition you have experienced.*

Interestingly, the key to your assignment can be found in the opposition you have experienced. There are clues to your future hidden in your past. It may seem like everything God has promised is not going to happen, but God is preparing you and positioning you. He is aligning you just as He did Joseph. He is moving you into your place of authority so the Kingdom of God can advance—through you.

*Therefore, brethren, be even more diligent to*

*make your call and election sure, for if you do these things you will never stumble; for so an entrance will be supplied to you abundantly into the everlasting kingdom of our Lord and Savior Jesus Christ* (2 Peter 1:10-11).

## GETTING IN POSITION

If you are not positioned in your proper seat of authority, you will never be able to fulfill your divine assignment—you will never fulfill the vision that God has placed in your heart.

- What mindsets are keeping you from taking your seat of authority?
- What is keeping you from stepping out into the realm of authority that will position you to fulfill your assignment?

Your seat is not about you. Your seat is about God's eternal purpose and the divine assignment He has entrusted to you.

- Pray for a prophetic revelation of your divine assignment within the eternal purpose of God.

- How will understanding God's eternal purpose for your existence affect how you deal with adversity?

The key to your assignment can be found in the opposition you have experienced. There are clues to your future hidden in your past.

- How have the hardships you've endured shaped you? What keys to victory have they given you?

Much of the opposition in your life is not about you, it's about your assignment. This is why God wants you to learn to exercise your authority and take dominion over the things He has placed in your care.

- Take an inventory of what God has placed in your care. How have you exercised your authority in those areas?

# CHAPTER 2

# JOURNEY TO AUTHORITY

*I will ascend into heaven,*
*I will exalt my throne above the*
*stars of God;*
*I will also sit on the mount*
*of the congregation*
*on the farthest sides of the north;*
*I will ascend above the heights*
*of the clouds,*
*I will be like the Most High*
(Isaiah 14:13-14).

Let me take you on an epic journey—back before the dawn of time when the race for the seat of authority began. We will have to go back to pre-history, to an age before the world was created. This was a time when God's most magnificent created being brought such honor and glory to God that he was seated above every other heavenly creature. He was beautiful. The music he brought forth was glorious. What a sight he was—and what an amazing sound he brought forth! Lucifer was as close to conveying the glory and splendor of God as any created being had ever been.

From Isaiah 14, we learn the importance of being seated in authority and how it was that lucifer aspired to occupy the highest seat of all. Lucifer already occupied a throne; he was already positioned in a very high place of authority. But pride caused him to desire a higher position still. He became determined to exalt his throne even *"above the stars of God"* (Isa. 14:13). He determined to *"ascend above the heights of the clouds"* (Isa. 14:14).

Everything we read that lucifer says in his heart is about ascending. He wanted to ascend into Heaven; he wanted his throne to ascend above the stars of God. Then he said, *"I will ascend above the heights of the clouds, I will be like the Most High"* (Isa. 14:14). Lucifer was after God's seat of authority. When he looked at his own beauty, when he looked at all that God had given him, there was one thing he didn't have that he knew was more important than everything else—a higher seat of authority. And the highest seat of authority in Heaven was the seat of God the Father, the Most High.

Lucifer was an archangel like Gabriel and Michael. Commanding angelic forces is the primary function of an archangel, but there is also a secondary duty. For example in Ezekiel 28, we read that lucifer was exceptionally beautiful. He had pipes and timbrels that brought forth beautiful sounds in the worship of God. He was an anointed cherub. He had a prestigious position in the Kingdom. He was an archangel, who had a throne—a place of authority over one third of Heaven's angels. He tasted how good it was to be in this place of power and authority and he wanted more.

In Ezekiel 28:14 we read that lucifer was "the anointed cherub who covers," and that God established him "on the holy mountain of God" where he "walked back and forth in the midst of fiery stones." When Ezekiel refers to lucifer as "the anointed cherub who covers," the word *covers* here gives us insight into "the assignment or task he was anointed for." While the archangel Gabriel was anointed to bring revelation, and Michael was anointed to bring strength, lucifer was anointed to bring a covering. But what does that mean? And what does that have to do with walking back and forth in the midst of the fiery stones?

We can find a clue to the significance of this in Isaiah chapter 6. Here we read about the prophet Isaiah who was taken up to Heaven where he *"saw the Lord sitting on a throne, high and lifted up"* (Isa. 6:1). There were coals of fire before the throne and, when he sees them, Isaiah says to the Lord, *"I am a man of unclean lips"* (Isa. 6:5). Then an angel comes and takes a coal of fire and sanctifies his lips.

> *Then one of the seraphim flew to me, having in his hand a live coal which he had taken with the tongs from the altar. And he touched my mouth with it, and said: "Behold, this has touched your lips; your iniquity is taken away, and your sin purged"* (Isaiah 6:6-7).

Now lucifer had been anointed to do this as the "cherub that covers." In Hebrew, the word *cover* used in Ezekiel means, "to form a protective screen of light and energy." A modern-day example of this would be an electric converter that can take 120 volts of electricity and change it into 12 volts so the device it is powering doesn't

*God is the Father of glory, and that glory is continually proceeding forth from His throne.*

blow up. Remember, God is the Father of glory, and that glory is continually proceeding forth from His throne. This glory—or energy—would burn up all of Heaven if it weren't for the living creatures we read about in Ezekiel chapter 1. Ezekiel describes these living creatures as follows:

> *The living beings looked like bright coals of fire or brilliant torches, and lightning seemed to flash back and forth among them. And the living beings darted to and fro like flashes of lightning. As I looked at these beings, I saw four wheels touching the ground beside them, one wheel belonging to each. The wheels sparkled as if made of beryl. All four wheels looked alike and were made the same; each wheel had a second wheel turning crosswise within it* (Ezekiel 1:13-16 NLT).

These four living creatures are constantly moving back and forth before the throne of God absorbing—or filtering—the energy emanating from God. They are Heaven's glory-handling mechanism. Although the Bible does not specifically describe this, I believe that during times when lucifer would be leading worship and the heart of God would be so deeply touched that waves of glory would be released, lucifer himself would become like a mirrored shield reflecting God's glory back to Him, protecting all of the inhabitants of Heaven. Lucifer would be engulfed in the power and raw energy of the glory of God. He became like a transmitter reflecting the light coming out of God seated on the throne of glory.

All of this light, all of God's glory, was moving through lucifer. He touched and tasted God's glory and finally aspired to *become* that glory! He dove for the seat of the Most High God—and fell. He coveted God's seat of authority, God's throne of glory, and the next thing we know he falls from Heaven to the earth like lightning falls from the sky—at 186,000 feet per second.

## THE SEAT OF MAN

*What is man that You are mindful of him, and the son of man that You visit him? For You have made him a little lower than the angels, and You have crowned him with glory and honor. You have made him to have dominion over the works of Your hands; You have put all things under his feet* (Psalm 8:4-6).

So now we move forward to Genesis and the making of man in God's own image. We learn that God gave man dominion over all the works of His hands. In other words, God gave Adam the highest seat of authority in the earth. He said to him, "Adam, since you're in charge, why don't you exercise your authority and name all of these animals?" Adam is given an assignment. But then we discover that although Adam is very busy, he is also very lonely. Important work is never a substitute for intimate companionship. So God provides a wife for Adam, and together they are put in charge of the Garden.

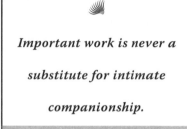

*Important work is never a substitute for intimate companionship.*

Adam and Eve are walking in close companionship with each other and with their God. There is unity and authority and peace for a time. But there is also a fallen angel in the earth. He has lost his seat of authority and is desperately looking for another one. The only person other than God in a position to delegate such a seat is Adam. Adam has the highest seat of authority on the planet, and satan wants it. He doesn't ask for it. He doesn't fight for it. He *steals* it! He tricks Adam into relinquishing it to him legally. Just as Esau gave up his birthright for a bite of stew, so Adam gave up his birthright for a bite of fruit.

Satan begins this epic deception by smooth-talking Eve. He seduces her by saying, "Look at this beautiful piece of fruit! How could something so beautiful be harmful? If you could taste this fruit it would open your mind to new wonders! Expand your horizons—become like God—take a bite!"

And so she looked at the fruit and said, "Wow, this *is* beautiful." It drew her attention. She could not resist taking a hold of it. She turned it over in her hand, looked at it longingly, and showed it to Adam. Together, they disobeyed God and ate of it. They violated their covenant and fell short of God's glory. Adam had been crowned with honor and glory, but because

> *Just as Esau gave up his birthright for a bite of stew, so Adam gave up his birthright for a bite of fruit.*

he did not honor God he lost his crown. He lost his seat of authority. Satan successfully usurped his seat and from that day forward became the "god of this world."

So it was all about a seat. Lucifer went for God's seat of authority and lost his own seat in the process. He then sought man's seat of authority and in the process caused Adam to break covenant with God. When Adam surrendered his seat to satan, he forfeited mankind's dominion and authority. He no longer ruled and reigned over all the earth and everything in it. In fact, he was expelled from Paradise. He became a transient, an impoverished wanderer looking for food. But God had a plan to reinstate humanity. Satan would not succeed in thwarting the eternal purposes of God.

## TEMPORARY REASSIGNMENT

*And the Lord God said, "The man has now become like one of Us, knowing good and evil. He must not be allowed to reach out his hand and take also from the tree of life and eat, and live forever." So the Lord God banished him from the Garden of Eden to work the ground from which he had been taken* (Genesis 3:22-23 NIV).

Let's go back to Genesis 3:8-10 where Adam and Eve first became aware of their exposed condition. When they heard the voice of the Lord, they were afraid because of their nakedness and hid themselves from God. "Where are you?" God called out. Since that time, mankind has been lost! Man has suffered from a lack of eternal purpose—a lack of understanding of where he is and why he is here—like in a bad dream, when you find yourself lost and naked in aisle nine at the grocery store, trying to hide your nakedness behind the evaporated milk display. In your shame and panic, you will do anything to hide yourself—anything to clear your name. This is the scene we find in Genesis chapter 3.

In Genesis 3:11, God asks, "Who told you that you were naked? Have you eaten from the tree of which I commanded you that you should not eat?"

In verse 12 Adam answers, "The woman whom You gave to be with me, she gave me of the tree, and I ate."

And so God said to the woman, "What is this you have done?" And the woman said, "The serpent deceived me, and I ate" (Gen. 3:13). And the buck was passed around the circle. By the time it got to the serpent, the Lord said in anger, "Because you have done this, you are cursed more than all cattle, and more than every beast of the field; on your belly you shall go, and you shall eat dust all the days of your life." Now listen to this first prophetic statement concerning mankind when the Lord says, "I will put enmity between you and the woman, and between your seed and her Seed; He shall bruise your head, and you shall bruise His heel" (Gen. 3:14-15).

Here God speaks in a prophetic language. He tells satan that the "Seed" of the woman will bruise his head. Why does God use the word *head* here? In Hebrew, the word *head* denotes a place of supreme governing authority. God is revealing that the authority satan stole from Adam is not going to keep the Seed of Adam from knocking him upside the head and taking it back. There is going to be some violence involved. The Seed of the woman is going to be an action hero—a lethal weapon as far as satan is concerned—who will knock him off his rocker of authority. There will be a new sheriff who shows up, knocks satan out of his saddle, and takes back His rightful place as the head of law enforcement.

So satan is a fugitive. He knows the Woman's Seed is destined to crush his head and take back headship of the earth. So when Adam has sons, satan puts murder in Cain's heart and he kills his brother Abel. What was satan doing? He was eliminating the seed. But Adam's family continues to grow so that eight generations later we have Noah. The Bible says that, *"Noah found favor* [grace] *in the eyes of the Lord,"* and that he *"was a righteous man, blameless among the people of his time"* (Gen. 6:8-9 NIV).

It is in this passage of Scripture that we also learn about the prevailing wickedness in the world. We learn that the sons of God took the daughters of men as their wives and bore children. (See Genesis 6:1-6.) They perverted the seed. Satan figured that if he could pervert the seed of humanity, he could prevent the prophecy from being fulfilled. We see the seed become so increasingly perverted that the sin and corruption cause God to regret ever having created it. He sends all the filth down the proverbial drain with one Great Flood. As a result, every wicked person is destroyed and all that remains is the righteous seed found in Noah and his family. God makes a fresh new start in the earth.

So now Noah's assignment is to replenish the earth. Another eight generations later, faithful Abraham enters the scene. God separates Abraham out from the nations of the earth and makes a covenant with him. This is when we see God's promise for you and I begin to take shape. God tells Abraham that through his Seed all of the people of the earth will be blessed. Notice he says "Seed" singular. This is the significance of the genealogy of Jesus being traced back to Abraham. The promise begins to take shape here with Abraham.

## JESUS TAKES HIS SEAT

*According to the working of His mighty power which He worked in Christ when He raised Him from the dead and seated Him at His right hand in the heavenly places, far above all principality and power and might and dominion, and every name that*

*is named, not only in this age but also in
that which is to come* (Ephesians 1:19b-21).

You and I are not just at the beginning of something; we
are the fulfillment of something that has been going on since
the beginning of time. In the New Testament, we read that
God's Anointed One, Christ Jesus, the Passover Lamb, the
King of kings, and Lord of Lords—the Savior of the world—
was born of a virgin. Gabriel appears on the scene to tell
Mary that she will conceive a baby when the power of the
Most High comes upon her. (See Luke 1:26-38.) Whenever
we see the words "Most High" in the Bible, we know it is
referring to God's supreme authority—or an eternal sovereign purpose of the Lord. God's sovereign and eternal purpose was taking place. Mary responded to this by saying,
*"Let it be to me according to your word"* (Luke 1:38).

Mary was impregnated with the Word of God
because by faith she received and conceived the Word of
God within herself, and it became flesh. The Word of
God was born and dwelt among us in the person of Jesus
Christ. The Word of God was on assignment. This Word
did not fail to do the thing God sent it to accomplish. In
Isaiah 55:11 God tells us, *"My word...shall not return to
Me void, but it shall accomplish what I please, and it shall
prosper in the thing for which I sent it."* Jesus is carrying
out the thing God sent Him to do.

Now Jesus found Himself in the synagogue reading from the Book of Isaiah. In Luke 4:16-19 we read how He was *"handed the book of the prophet Isaiah"* and began reading from the first verse of chapter 61:

> *The Spirit of the Lord is upon Me, because He has anointed Me to preach the gospel to the poor; He has sent Me to heal the brokenhearted, to proclaim liberty to the captives and recovery of sight to the blind, to set at liberty those who are oppressed; to proclaim the acceptable year of the Lord* (Luke 4:18-19).

As was the custom, there was a predetermined section of reading scheduled for this particular day in the synagogue. This is why the Book of Isaiah was handed to Jesus. Then we read, *"He closed the book, and gave it back to the attendant and sat down. And the eyes of all who were in the synagogue were fixed on Him. And He began to say to them, 'Today this Scripture is fulfilled in your hearing'"* (Luke 4:20-21). In other words, what He did was sit down in the Messiah Seat. Every eye was fixed upon Him because Jesus did not return to the seat He had been sitting in before, but He sat down in the seat reserved for the coming Messiah.

In those days, a special chair was kept empty at all times at the front of the synagogue. It was believed that one day the Messiah would take His place of authority by sitting down in this hallowed seat—and that is exactly what Jesus did. Jesus was saying, "The hand of the sovereign Lord is upon *Me* because He has anointed *Me*." The congregation believed He was simply reading a passage of Scripture from the Book of Isaiah and were astonished when He sat down in the seat reserved for the Messiah. As every eye was fixed upon Him sitting in this seat, He declared, *"Today this Scripture is fulfilled in your hearing"* (Luke 4:21).

This word came from the heart of God. This was a word having to do with God's sovereign eternal purpose that had been spoken of by the prophets of old. But now, *this* was the appointed time; this was the day; and all who were present were hearing and watching this *kairos* moment in time.

In the hearing of those who grew up with Him, who knew His parents and siblings, there in front of His neighbors in His hometown of Nazareth, Jesus read prophetic Scripture and then sat down saying, *"The*

> *As every eye was fixed upon Him sitting in this seat, He declared,* "Today this Scripture is fulfilled in your hearing"

*Scripture you've just heard has been fulfilled this very day!"* (Luke 4:21 NLT). Now we can understand why it is that these people were so compelled to grab hold of this audacious young Man, drag Him out of town, and attempt to throw Him off the nearest cliff! But then we read that Jesus passed right through them and went on His way. (See Luke 4:28-30.)

For every assignment there is a corresponding seat of authority. Jesus in this moment is functioning from His place of authority. He is literally untouchable as the hand of the Lord is now truly upon Him. Once you sit in your destined place of authority the Hand of God comes upon you. Prior to this moment, these folks could have done anything to Jesus, but something changed when He sat in His seat and made the declaration, "The Spirit of the sovereign Lord is upon Me." Something shifted when He sat down in His place of authority and declared, "The hand of the Lord is upon Me, the corporate hand, the sovereign hand—which is the Spirit of God—is upon Me so that I can fulfill My divine assignment on the earth!" Jesus stepped up to another level of power and authority once

> *Jesus stepped up to another level of power and authority once He sat down in His seat and placed Himself under the hand of God.*

He sat down in His seat and placed Himself under the hand of God.

Interestingly, we read in Luke 4:14 that before He even began to approach His seat, before He was even close to the synagogue, Jesus *"returned in the power of the Spirit."* Why was He *"in the power of the Spirit"* for a duration of time *prior* to taking His seat? Because that was the power He would need to enable Him to get there. Often we find that we are operating in the power of the Spirit and don't understand the purpose for it, so we "mis-steward" the power. But this power is an individual power that comes upon your life to help propel you toward your proper place in God's plan. It was an individual power that came upon Jesus in the season prior to the moment He took His seat in the synagogue—not the corporate power He would need to fulfill His assignment.

This personal power helped Him pass the tests in the desert. It was a personal empowerment that helped Him resist temptation and gave Him the discernment and wisdom He needed to move forward. It was after He came out of the wilderness that God led Him to His seat of authority. Once He sat down in that place, the corporate hand of God would render Him immune to any spiritual or physical opposition.

Every type of empowerment is for a purpose. There is a type of power needed to get you to your seat—to your place of authority—and another type of power that will enable you to fulfill your assignment once you are sitting in that place of authority. You will walk in a certain degree of power in order to prepare, grow, and move toward your seat—and another degree of power altogether to finish the race. This corporate power is not about you; it is about fulfilling your assignment and advancing God's eternal purposes.

Jesus was called, anointed, gifted, and appointed. But He needed to have a seat. From this seat He goes on to the cross, sheds His blood, and dies for the sins of the world. From this seat He goes to the grave and rises again, the firstborn of many, ascending to His seat at the right hand of the Father. We are told in Ephesians and Colossians that we have been made alive together with Him—raised up together with Him and seated with Him in heavenly places far above any other power or authority. What has Jesus accomplished? He has given you and I a seat of authority!

## SEATED WITH CHRIST

*But God, who is rich in mercy…made us alive together with Christ…and raised us up together, and made us sit together in the heavenly places in Christ Jesus* (Ephesians 2:4-6).

In Colossians, we see Genesis 3:15 starting to take place. In Colossians 2:13 we are told that *"being dead in* [our] *trespasses and the uncircumcision of* [our] *flesh"* we had no idea what Jesus was doing. But Paul tells us in Colossians 2:14-15 that Jesus has made us alive together with Him, *"Having wiped out the handwriting of requirements that was against us, which was contrary to us.... having nailed it to the cross. Having disarmed principalities and powers, He made a public spectacle of them, triumphing over them in it."*

So while Jesus is on the cross, not only is He redeeming us, but our sin nature is also being crucified. Then it says that we are buried with Him. This is what baptism represents. Through faith and obedience we publicly demonstrate what took place in the death, burial, and resurrection of Christ. Through the work of the cross, we too are crucified, we die, and are buried. The old man was crucified in Christ. But the best part is that we have been regenerated. We are reborn. We are rebirthed! We are a new creation. Paul says in Galatians 2:20, "I have been crucified with Christ; it is no longer I who live, but Christ lives in me; and the life which I now live in the flesh I live by faith in the Son of God."

Today in Christ, we are a new origin of species—a species that never existed before. As Noah was after the flood—given a fresh start in a new place with a clean slate—you and I are a new species walking this earth. But a new species requires a new seat of authority. God didn't plan to give this new species the same seat that Adam had. He basically says, "Listen, you new species, you new creation; I'm not just going to give you a seat of authority over the dominion of the works of My hand—I'm going to give you a higher seat of authority. I'm going to seat you in Christ on My right hand! I'll share My seat with you."

> *Today in Christ, we are a new origin of species—a species that never existed before.*

Now, remember, that's the seat lucifer was after. God said He would prepare a banquet for us in front of our enemies—and that is what He has done. Satan is eating his heart out because after all of that striving for the best seat, here we are seated with Christ at the right hand of the Father! There isn't any better place we could be seated in the universe!

## SEATED IN MERCY

*But God, who is rich in mercy, because of His great love with which He loved us... made us sit together in the heavenly places in Christ Jesus, that in the ages to come He might show the exceeding riches of His grace in His kindness toward us in Christ Jesus* (Ephesians 2:4,6-7).

Even though we celebrate this wonderful position we have in Christ, we misunderstand the final purpose. The purpose for which He seated you and I in heavenly places was so that *"in the ages to come He might show the exceeding riches of His grace in His kindness toward us in Christ Jesus."* This is His eternal purpose—God's ultimate end goal.

The first Adam chose to break covenant with God and to give his authority over to satan. On the one hand, while lucifer was sentenced to burn forever in the lake of fire as a result of his rebellion, Adam is forgiven. This rebellious man who sins against God—who betrays his Maker—is whom God chooses to redeem!

Not only that, but God goes so far as to make this old man Adam a new creation in Christ. God says, "I'm not into evolution. I'm not going to evolve you from a bad guy to a good guy. Forget the growing pains. I'm going to do away with the old sinful nature and make you a brand-new creature!" So this new species shows up and God says, "Hey new species, let me tell you something. I'm going to seat you on My right hand here with Christ and show you My exceeding grace and mercy." All the while, the enemy is looking at you and fuming! Satan is furious because you were given *as a gift* a seat higher than he could ever have, even above the first Adam who lost his seat of authority over all of the earth. That first Adam wasn't seated on the right hand of God, but you and I have been seated there in the last Adam.

There are some of you who are working very hard to get promoted; you are striving and trying to get blessed. Some of you are asking, "Where's my provision? Why aren't I walking in all of the blessings God has promised me?" You must realize that for every assignment there is a seat or place of authority reserved for you. The question is, are you seated in it? This is where you will find your blessing and provision. God will also promote you to a greater seat of authority and increase your influence and power as you are responsible and faithful to the seat He has entrusted you to.

> *There is a seat or place of authority reserved for you. The question is, are you seated in it?*

Look again at Ephesians 1:3: "Blessed be the God and Father of our Lord Jesus Christ, who has blessed us with every spiritual blessing *in the heavenly places* in Christ." The blessing is in your seat—in the heavenly places in Christ! The blessing is found in that high place where you are positioned in Christ. Now if you aren't seated in that place, you aren't going to be walking in all of the blessings that God has promised—but worse, you won't be able to fulfill your assignment on the earth.

Don't take the high road; take the high seat!

*Beloved, I pray that you may prosper in all things and be in health, just as your soul prospers* (3 John 1:2).

## GETTING IN POSITION

Adam had the highest seat of authority on the planet when satan tricked him into legally relinquishing it to him.

- Has the enemy ever tricked you out of your seat? Have you ever felt like Esau who gave up his birthright for a bite of stew when you give up your authority in Christ for some carnal desire?
- How can you keep the enemy from stealing your authority on a day-to-day basis?
- "Most High" in the Bible refers to God's supreme authority—or an eternal sovereign purpose of the Lord.

God's sovereign and eternal purpose took place when the "power of the Most High" came upon Mary in Luke 1:35.

- Would you be able to respond as Mary did by saying, "Let it be to me according to Your word" (Luke 1:38). Will you allow yourself to be impregnated with the Word—or the will—of God?

When Jesus returned from being tempted in the wilderness, He went to the synagogue, read from the Book of Isaiah, and sat down in His place of authority declaring, "The Spirit of God is upon me so that I can fulfill my divine assignment on the earth."

- After you return from your season of "being tempted," will you be able to sit down in your place of authority and declare, "The Spirit of God is upon me to fulfill my part in God's eternal plan?" Why or why not?
- What is God's eternal purpose—His ultimate end goal? (See Ephesians 2:7.)

CHAPTER 3

# POSITIONED FOR BLESSING

*We are on our way to the place the Lord
promised us, for He said, "I will give it to
you." Come with us…for the Lord has
promised wonderful blessings for Israel!*
(Numbers 10:29 NLT)

So many times in our life we're looking for the blessings of the Lord. *Blessings*—notice that is plural, meaning "acts in the natural realm that are in alignment with the favor of the Lord for His people." The blessing of the Lord is spiritual. It is an empowerment in the Spirit that comes upon us, which then releases manifestations of the blessings—or the grace—of God in our lives. Wherever we are in life, we're looking for the blessing of the Lord to be in operation.

71

When you have God's blessing operating in your life, even unbelievers will take notice and begin to ask questions. The blessing on a believer's life bears witness to the reality of God. God blessed Israel for this reason. The nations surrounding Israel could not avoid seeing the evidence of the blessing of the Lord on God's people. They were compelled to exclaim, "Truly, we see the God of Israel at work!" God is always at work—and His heart has always been to release blessing upon His children.

If you are a believer, the blessing of God may already be upon you, but perhaps you haven't known how to appropriate its effect in your natural life. In this chapter I will share some keys from the Scriptures on how to do that. Let's begin by looking at how Abraham positioned himself—and all of his descendants—to receive God's favor and blessing. Look at this foundational passage in Galatians 3:7-14:

> **Therefore know that only those who are of faith are sons of Abraham.** *And the Scripture, foreseeing that God would justify the Gentiles by faith, preached the gospel to Abraham beforehand, saying, "In you all the nations shall be blessed." So then those who are of faith are blessed with believing Abraham. For as many as are of*

*the works of the law are under the curse;*
*for it is written, "Cursed is everyone who*
*does not continue in all things which are*
*written in the book of the law, to do them."*
*But that no one is justified by the law in*
*the sight of God is evident, for **"the just***
***shall live by faith."** Yet the law is not of*
*faith, but "the man who does them shall*
*live by them." Christ has redeemed us from*
*the curse of the law, having become a curse*
*for us (for it is written, "Cursed is everyone*
*who hangs on a tree"), that the blessing of*
*Abraham might come upon the Gentiles in*
*Christ Jesus, that we might receive the*
*promise of the Spirit through faith.*

Notice the verse that states, *"The just shall live by faith."* And then look again at verse 9: *"Those who are of faith are blessed with believing Abraham."* There is a connection between living by faith and being blessed. One of the keys to walking in God's blessing is having the faith of "believing Abraham"—a faith that simply believes God.

## POSITIONED BY FAITH

*Therefore it is of faith that it might be*

*according to grace, so that the promise might be sure to all the seed, not only to those who are of the law, but also to those who are of the faith of Abraham, who is the father of us all.... being fully convinced that what He had promised He was also able to perform. And therefore "it was accounted to him for righteousness"* (Romans 4:16,21-22).

Proverbs 10:6 tells us that, *"Blessings are on the head of the righteous."* Therefore if we expect blessings, we must be counted among the righteous. So what is the connection between living by faith and being blessed? The connection lies in the central truth of the New Testament: that those who by faith believe God's Word concerning Christ are made righteous and that righteousness is a gift of God that can only be received by faith: *"For by grace you have been saved through faith, and that not of yourselves; it is the gift of God"* (Eph. 2:8).

In Galatians 3:6 and Romans 4:22, we learn that God counted Abraham righteous as a result of his faith. In other words, he was found faithful, not perfect; he was counted righteous because he believed God. He believed God enough to trust and therefore obey Him. In Hebrews 11:8 we are told that God called Abraham to go to a place he knew nothing about; he didn't even know how to get there. Many times this is the kind of faith we are asked to walk in. God directs you to head in a completely foreign direction—but once you step out in faith, you learn how to trust God. God wants you to trust Him with all of your heart, and until you do, you will never be in a position to receive God's greatest bless-ings for your life. And that is because until you fully trust Him, you will never fully obey Him.

*Trusting God means that you do things you don't necessarily understand with your mind.*

Trusting God means that you do things you don't nec-essarily understand with your mind. You are willing to fol-low God's instructions, even when they don't make sense. Faith is not something you can rationalize or calculate—it is something you decide to believe out of a trusting heart.

> *Trust in the Lord with all your heart, and lean not on your own understanding; in all your ways acknowledge Him, and He shall direct your paths* (Proverbs 3:5-6).

Righteousness is a result of faith, and faith requires

that you trust God. If you believe God is really in control and working on your behalf, then you will be empowered to follow an invisible path to an unknown place. This level of faith demands a type of blind obedience. But those who walk in this kind of faith are not really blind at all. They see the truth about who they are in Christ; they are able to see with their spiritual eyes. They are also able to hear with spiritual ears. When they hear the voice of the Holy Spirit, they obey, knowing that their blessing does not depend on seeing where they are going in the natural, but on knowing where they are headed in the spirit.

## FAITH REQUIRES OBEDIENCE

*Has the Lord as great delight in burnt offerings and sacrifices, as in obeying the voice of the Lord? Behold, to obey is better than sacrifice, and to heed than the fat of rams (1 Samuel 15:22).*

Many times people substitute sacrifice for obeying God. They tell of their great sacrifices and forget about diligently obeying God. I am not saying that in the journey to fulfilling your assignment you won't have to go through sacrifices but if your walking in disobedience your sacrifices mean nothing. In the Old Testament under the law the concept of obedience was entirely about obeying the law; it was a representation of a performance-based legalism. In the New Testament, obedience is a representation of faith. It is a spiritual revelation that produces the heart-faith necessary for you to obey God. When God asks you to do something, it requires a living faith rooted in your heart—and when out of that faith you obey Him, you are positioning yourself for blessing.

*He is talking about living your life as a representation of obeying an invisible God who speaks to you and guides you and directs you—a perpetual posture of obedience that requires a continually growing faith*

You have often heard people say, "I live by faith." But the kind of faith I am talking about is not simply "believing God" for rent money. When God tells you, "The just shall live by faith," He is talking about living your life as a representation of obeying an invisible God who speaks to you and guides you and directs you—a perpetual posture of obedience that requires a continually growing faith.

I have a pastor friend who felt led to pioneer a church, while at the same time feeling called to continue working as a corporate consultant. He was in a quandary because he couldn't reconcile pioneering a church with remaining in the marketplace. "I don't feel like I'm really living my faith like you are because you travel full time and have stepped out. God spoke to you and you stepped out of the corporate world," he confided to me. "Here I am in the corporate world and I'm also in the church, and now I'm wondering if I'm really living by faith."

> *As long as you are sure that it's Him, that it's God guiding you and leading you and directing you, even though you can't see the path, you are positioning yourself for blessing in your life.*

Here is a man diligently pursuing God's will, obeying what he hears God telling him to do, and wondering if he is being faithful. He is questioning his faith walk because it doesn't look exactly the same as others who are "walking by faith." I told him that living and walking by faith is a matter of obeying God. Since he obeyed God's call to remain in the marketplace—regardless of what it *looked like* he should do—He was walking in faith.

You have to obey God in whatever area He is calling you as an individual. You can't copy someone else and expect to get blessed because they did. You can learn from their obedience and be encouraged and inspired by their faith. They stepped out and obeyed what they heard God telling them to do, and if they were able to hear and obey, so can you. You can hear the voice of God for yourself and walk in the personal thing He is giving to you, and that's the key. As long as you are obeying God, you are living by faith, and because you are believing, trusting, and obeying Him, the blessing of the Lord is upon you.

You have to obey God in the thing that He is calling you to do. The blessing of the Lord is always connected to a faith that says, "I will obey You, Lord, even though it doesn't make sense, even though I don't understand it." As long as you are sure that it's Him, that it's God guiding you and leading you and directing you, even though you can't see the path, you are positioning yourself for blessing in your life.

## SEEING THE INVISIBLE

*...Even though our outward man is perishing, yet the inward man is being renewed day by day.... While we do not look at the things which are seen, but at the things which are not seen. For the things which are seen are temporary, but*

79

*the things which are not seen are eternal*
(2 Corinthians 4:16,18).

One time the Lord said to me, "Faith is seeing the invisible." I told the Lord I needed some Scripture. I was trying to make sense of this. The Lord reminded me about Second Corinthians 4:18, which says, in essence, "The things that are seen are temporal and subject to change but the things which are unseen are eternal." And He began to deal with me about Hebrews 11:1, *"Now faith is the substance of things hoped for, the evidence of things not seen."* In other words, the Spirit began to explain to me, "When you have faith it's actually the substance of something that already exists in the spirit realm. Faith is the substance of something real, even if it is unseen."

When we talk about faith, we are talking about the evidence of something that actually exists in the unseen realm. That is why we do not walk by our natural sight but by faith or seeing the invisible. That's why when you begin to follow the leading of the Spirit and obey Him in the area He's directing you, no matter how difficult it sounds, no matter how crazy it sounds, you'll begin moving closer to that sovereign place where the blessing of the Lord begins to increase and continues to multiply.

Many of you are in possession of the promises of God. You have been redeemed from the curse of the law and are seated in heavenly places in Christ Jesus. But although you have the promise legally, you're not walking in the full manifestation of that promise. Deuteronomy 28:1-2 says, *"Now it shall come to pass, if you diligently obey the voice of the Lord your God* [there's that voice, there's that leading again], *to observe carefully all His commandments which I command you today* [present tense, that He is commanding you *today*], *that the Lord your God will* [watch this] *set you high above all nations of the earth. And all these blessings* [plural] *shall come upon you and overtake you, because you obey the voice of the Lord your God."*

There are two things I want you to notice in this verse beyond the obvious of hearing the voice of God and diligently obeying His voice. First, it says that God will set you on high. Before you see the manifestation of blessings, God will set you "high above all nations." He has to set you in a place of authority so the blessings can begin to overtake you. This is not about you chasing blessings. There may be a season in your life where it seems all you're doing is chasing a blessing. But the key is to get to that place where blessings are chasing you. Once you get

> *He has to set you in a place of authority so the blessings can begin to overtake you.*

into that place, then wherever you go, the blessing of the Lord overtakes you.

Second, you must be able to identify the source of those blessings. How can you know you are in the right place and that it is the blessing of the Lord chasing you? You will know because you will see more of God's sovereignty in it. Don't you love it when God blesses your socks off and you didn't have anything to do with it? You'll know it's the sovereignty of God blessing you when you didn't strive for it, you didn't fight for it, you didn't wrestle somebody down for it, and you didn't run somebody over with your car. The blessing was unexpected, undeserved, and above what you ever asked or imagined. You know that blessing is of God! Doesn't it give you a sense of peace and comfort knowing that God is at work in your life? You are able to relax as you rest in that knowledge.

But the key is being seated in a position of authority—stepping into that place of authority that God has for your life. The blessing is always connected to the seat or place of authority that God has established for you. That's why we read in Proverbs 10:6 KJV, *"Blessings are upon the head of the just,"* and in Hebrews 10:38, *"The just shall live by faith."* So these blessings come into your life and begin to overtake you because you're seated in that place of authority to fulfill your assignment. As you begin to identify your seat of authority and occupy those areas where God has granted you dominion, as you are faithful and obedient in that place, God will bless you!

As long as you are obeying God, He is connecting you to your place of authority. Let's look again at Ephesians 1:3 where Paul prays, *"Blessed be the God and Father of our Lord Jesus Christ, who has blessed us with every spiritual blessing in the heavenly places in Christ."* So where are the blessings that belong to you? They are in the heavenlies; they are located in the high places. They are actually located in the seat where you and I have been seated in Christ Jesus, on the right hand of the Father. That's where the blessings are; they are not down here. You obtain access to them when you are seated in your place of

> *As you begin to identify your seat of authority and occupy those areas where God has granted you dominion, as you are faithful and obedient in that place, God will bless you!*

authority in Christ. There are two dimensions of this place of authority. The first is your personal place of authority as a believer and the second is the corporate seat of authority which relates to your assignment in God's eternal purposes. You must recognize where the

Father has positioned you, and though you might not see this place with your natural eye, you can spiritually discern it. Your place of authority first exists in the heavenlies; it is unseen and eternal. It is the substance of all you've hoped for.

## FROM WHERE BLESSING FLOWS

*By the God of your father who will help you, and by the Almighty who will bless you with blessings of heaven above...* (Genesis 49:25).

Blessings flow from the top down. That's the way of God. *"Every good gift and every perfect gift is from above, and comes down from the Father of lights..."* (James 1:17). Blessings flow downward from the Father. Because the blessing comes from above, the first thing God does is make you alive in Christ; He raises you up and then makes you sit in heavenly places so that you can be positioned to prosper—positioned to flow in the blessings of the Lord according to the empowerment of His blessing.

Faith begins by embracing what God has freely provided in the form of righteousness. Faith and righteousness are always connected. That's why Romans 1:17 says,

*"...The righteousness of God is revealed from faith to faith...."* It is a progressive revelation of righteousness. This gift begins to go into operation as it is revealed to your heart. You continue to grow as the Word of God grows in you. You go from glory to glory as you are renewed day by day in your inner man. The righteousness of God acquired by faith is your passport into new territory. It allows you access into the Promised Land. It's your pathway into the place of promise that He has prepared for you.

That is the beginning of believing faith. This is the faith that recognizes that God has set you on high, seated you in Christ, and positioned you in a place of authority. The blessing flows from the Father to the Son, and from the Son it pours down through His Body. So the blessing always flows downward.

Faith believes that if you don't have what you've been promised in the current season, then it's coming in the next season; faith waits for the blessing to manifest "in due season." Faith says, "In due season God's going to do that thing," but then asks, "What is God telling me to do in this season?" What is God trying to teach you? What tests does He need you to pass so He can promote you to the place to which He has called you? There is place of promotion and a place of blessing if you remain faithful and obedient. If you yield to the voice of the Spirit and obey the promptings of the Lord, you will walk in that place of blessing and see the manifestation of God.

In Proverbs 10:22 we read, *"The blessing of the Lord makes one rich, and He adds no sorrow with it."* When you *strive* to get something, you will always have sorrow with it, and you'll know it's not the blessing of the Lord simply because it resulted from your own striving. Many times we take the promise of God and we try to make it come to pass. Well that's not the kind of blessing that overtakes you, and you know if you've ever done that, you're not happy about it inside. You don't experience the joy of God in it. But when God just blesses you, all you can do is humble yourself and bow down saying, "Father, thank You! Thank You so much! I appreciate You, I thank You!" You begin to understand how the blessing of God operates, and you step into it.

> *If you yield to the voice of the Spirit and obey the promptings of the Lord, you will walk in that place of blessing and see the manifestation of God.*

So instead of striving to obtain blessings, instead of forcing the promises of God, you should be resting. Many people think they are exercising their faith by over-obligating themselves, "suffering for a cause," or continually confessing, even sometimes shouting out the promises or yelling at the enemy until they are hoarse. Listen to this passage from Hebrews 4:2-3: *"For indeed the gospel was preached to us as well as to them; but the word which they heard did not profit them, not being mixed with faith in those who heard it.* **For we who have believed do enter that rest....**" Have you believed and entered into that rest?

Now look at Matthew 11:28 from The Message:

> *Are you tired? Worn out? Burned out on religion? Come to Me. Get away with Me and you'll recover your life. I'll show you how to take a real rest. Walk with Me and work with Me—watch how I do it. Learn the unforced rhythms of grace. I won't lay anything heavy or ill-fitting on you. Keep company with Me and you'll learn to live freely and lightly.*

The place of authority God calls you to is not meant to be burdensome. Obeying God never requires you to be anxious or stressed out. Jesus said, *"My yoke is easy and My burden is light"* (Matt. 11:30). Listen to the rest of Hebrews 4, *"There remains therefore a rest for the people of God. For he who has entered His rest has himself also ceased from his works as God did from His. Let us therefore be diligent to enter that rest, lest anyone fall according to the same example of disobedience"* (Heb. 4:9-11). If you are going to be obedient, you must be diligent to enter that rest.

A key to entering this place of rest and blessing is learning to sow to the spirit. Look at Galatians 6:8 (KJV): "For he that soweth to his flesh shall of the flesh reap corruption; but he that soweth to the Spirit shall of the Spirit reap life everlasting." When you sow to the carnal desires of your flesh nature to sin or do such things as not managing your time well, not eating right, not getting enough rest, etc.—you will reap corruption, just like if you try to obtain the blessings of God through your own strength and self-will. But if you sow to the Spirit—by yielding to the desires, promptings, or leadings of the Spirit—then of the Spirit you will reap life everlasting.

> *I began to get stronger and stronger in that area because I yielded to God's small promptings.*

So how do you do that in your life? You practice. You begin with the small things, and you begin when things are still small. Let's look at an example: If you have a city where there are only one or two murders, you can focus your law enforcement efforts in that area and do something about it. But when the situation gets to the point where murders are too numerous for law enforcement to handle, then you have a real problem. Crime escalates, you have rampant corruption, and now the criminal element seems to be in control. It works the same way when you yield to a carnal desire in your human nature; the more you yield to it, the more it takes control of you instead of you controlling it. The more you give way to those desires, the more corruption steps in and takes over. On the other hand, the more you yield to the promptings of the Spirit of God, in your spirit the more you'll begin to reap life everlasting.

There have been times I would begin to pray but didn't feel like praying. My flesh didn't want to pray. My flesh wanted to play or sleep or work, anything else but pray. But in those times I began to say to myself, "No, I'm going to yield," and when I felt the prompting I began to pray. The next time I got the prompting I yielded again. Then I got to the place where prayer became so enjoyable that I couldn't wait to pray. God began to give me a desire in my heart and "life everlasting" intensified in that area. I began to get stronger and stronger in that area because I yielded to God's small promptings.

## GETTING INTO GOD'S DOWNLINE

*Behold, how good and how pleasant it is for brethren to dwell together in unity! It is like the precious oil upon the head, running down on the beard, the beard of Aaron, running down on the edge of his garments. It is like the dew of Hermon, descending upon the mountains of Zion; for there the Lord commanded the blessing—life forevermore* (Psalm 133).

There are three things I want you to notice in Psalm 133. First, the Lord compares the *"goodness of brethren dwelling in unity"* with *"precious oil upon the head"* and *"the dew of Hermon."* Second, we are told that the oil, like the dew, flows downward: "running *down* the beard" and "*descending* upon the mountains." Third, and most important, the passage states that this is the place where God *"commanded the blessing."* It's the place of commanded blessing!

When God *commands* a blessing, that's major! Once God commands a blessing, nobody can touch it. This is essentially what God said to Abraham. He told Abraham that he and his descendants were blessed and that whoever blessed Abraham would be blessed and whoever cursed him would be cursed. You don't want to mess with somebody whom God has commanded a blessing upon. If you do, you are coming up against the command of God!

This is why in Deuteronomy 28:10 it states, *"All peoples of the earth shall see that you are called by the name of the Lord, and they shall be afraid of you."* When you understand the way authority works, and you step into a place where you position yourself under the hand of God, the sovereignty of the Lord comes upon your life. Many times we try to *position the hand* over us, but instead we are told to *position ourselves* under the hand of God. That's where the blessing is; that's where the spout is; that's where the blessing is

> *The closer you come under the hand of God, the more the blessings of the Lord will begin to overtake you.*

flowing out. This is the place where the Lord has commanded the blessing. When you come into this place, you come under the sovereignty of God and you begin to see the intensity of God's blessing. It always happens slowly and gradually. The closer you come under the hand of God, the more the blessings of the Lord will begin to overtake you.

This is really a matter of alignment. Getting aligned with how the Spirit is moving in the Body of Christ, dwelling in unity, and understanding lines of authority. Unity requires not only submitting to one another, but also to those in authority over us. The process of alignment begins with the Holy Spirit leading you. Are you able to submit to leading of the Spirit in every area of your life? The Spirit is attempting to lead you to the place where you enter into the center of God's plan—the eternal purpose He has foreordained for you. This is what you were wired for and what you were destined for—what you are graced and anointed for.

I have experienced this in my own life. For six years I sat under the teaching and authority of my pastor in Toronto. I cleaned up at the church and took out the garbage. I would be on television preaching one night and the next morning I would take the garbage out at the church. What was I doing? I was humbling myself before the "seat" of the man in authority over me. While I was humbling myself, the Lord showed me that the dew that was upon his head would become a river in my life. I inherited rivers that were the dew of other men's labor. I humbled myself before their seat of authority and was faithful to obey, even when it didn't look like it was working.

I knew that I had a special calling, yet even though God had spoken some things to me and had made some promises, for a while it didn't look like I was moving in that direction. But God was working in my life all the time. I can see now that it was all part of my training. I learned to take the garbage out of the church so I could *take the garbage out of the church!* Wherever I go, that's what I do. I'm a sanitation engineer. I show up with a sanitation truck and we have a Holy Ghost gutter clean out because that's what God wants to do!

I learned many things from my pastor. I learned things about ministry from him—but I also got something in the Spirit. A day came when by chance I found myself prophetically kneeling before his seat because there was no other place to sit. The Lord said to me, "You've passed the test and you will see!" And I have seen. All you have to do is pass your tests and you will get to your seat and that place of blessing. I know the exact times when I passed certain tests because the Holy Spirit spoke to me, saying, "You just passed that test! You're one step closer to My sovereign plan." To be first, you must be last. You must learn to humble yourself and submit if you want the Lord to exalt you.

> *All you have to do is pass your tests and you will get to your seat and that place of blessing.*

God is teaching us how the blessing flows from the top down. He has seated us in heavenly places because that's where all the spiritual blessings are. From there they flow into our lives and out of our lives into the lives of others. That's why God has ordained blessings in this way. The blessing is never meant for you to keep and lock up so that it never blesses anybody else. That would block the flow! You are simply a part of the blessing stream, or blessing channel. Your job is to keep your part of the channel clear and flowing. The true nature of blessing is found in Matthew 10:8, *"Freely you have received, freely give."*

It is the nature of the blessing you receive that compels you to want to give. By the time you grow into the place where you are positioned to receive the fullness of God's blessings, *who* you are spiritually will have been changed because you will have learned to yield and adapt to the nature of God. God's giving nature will have rubbed off on you, and you will want to see other people blessed. As the blessings increase in your life, this whole process is being worked out in your heart.

So here you are, and God begins to bring blessing. Because God's blessing is on you, everyone around you is going to get blessed. Look at what happened to Laban in the Old Testament. Laban realized the blessing was upon Jacob because he was the seed of Abraham and Isaac. He wanted to keep Jacob with him. He tried to capture Jacob so that he could use him to get blessed. But Jacob had also been a trickster, so ultimately he had to reap what he had sown. There came a day when Jacob wrestled with God, and do you remember what he said? He said, "I'm not going until You bless me!" He got to the place where he realized, "I need the blessing!" He told the "Man" that he wouldn't let Him go until he got the blessing—and he got blessed! His name was even changed—because by the time you enter that place of blessing even your identity will be changed. You will be renewed, and you will be transformed. (See Genesis 32:22-32.)

By the time you get to that place, you will have passed some tests and trials that will prove your heart and your motives. By the time you receive the blessing, you will have undergone some shifts in your mindset, and maybe your name will even be changed. The Man asked Jacob, "Who are you?" What an interesting question. Jacob replied, "This is who I am: My name is Jacob." The Man said, "No, you're not Jacob anymore." Can you imagine? That's the only identity he'd ever known! "Then who am I?" Jacob asked. The Man answered, "You are Israel, a prince who has prevailed

> *His name was even changed—because by the time you enter that place of blessing even your identity will be changed.*

with God." Something changed about Jacob, and the blessing of the Lord came upon him.

I believe there is a place in your life where you get tested and tried and you must position yourself by passing those tests in your life. You'll know when that empowerment takes on flesh in your life: when it's not just a Scripture that you're reading about yourself and it's not just something you've been promised, but it's something you now possess that was promised to you and set apart for you in Christ Jesus. When you possess it, then it starts to get fun! When you possess the promise set apart for you, then you begin to see God's sovereignty. That's how blessing works.

> *Once God commands a blessing upon your life, nothing in this world can prevail against you!*

Many times we think blessing is some gimmick. We determine to do some crazy thing—give somebody some money and buy some blessing. That's not what it's about. It's about you obeying God and getting positioned under the hand of the Lord. And guess what happens? If any man comes against you, it avails nothing because man is not the source of your blessing. If the devil comes against you, it doesn't matter because the devil didn't bless you. Once

God commands a blessing upon your life, nothing in this world can prevail against you!

## IT'S NOT ABOUT YOU

*But the manifestation of the Spirit is given to each one for the profit of all* (1 Corinthians 12:7).

He wants to bless you because He wants to bless the people around you. There are people whose blessing is locked up in the authority God has woven into your life. There are people whose deliverance is locked up within your calling. Because the people you are called to touch and connect with and relate to are waiting on something you are carrying. You are the carrier of someone's deliverance; you are the carrier of someone's promise; you are the carrier of someone's victory. So when you say, "Lord, I don't want to be blessed," essentially what you are saying is that you don't care about any of those people whom you have been called to bless.

Look for ways to bless people. That's how you can know you're walking in the blessings of God, when you are actively looking for ways to bless people everywhere you go.The Bible says that if you're a parent, you should leave your children's children an inheritance or you are worse than an infidel, which is an unbeliever. (See Proverbs 13:22 and First Timothy 5:8.) If your mindset is, "Lord, bless my family of four and no more," that's not how it works. God wants you to be a blessing to the people around you. Look for ways to bless people. That's how you can know you're walking in the blessings of God, when you are actively looking for ways to bless people everywhere you go.

> *Look for ways to bless people. That's how you can know you're walking in the blessings of God, when you are actively looking for ways to bless people everywhere you go.*

When you get into a place of authority, you begin to realize that you're connecting to a corporate place. God wants to make *you* a corporate blessing. When you align yourself to authority—or submit yourself to the authority God has placed over you—God releases authority in your life, and the blessings of God begin to increase so that your power to bless increases. Just as God told Abraham in Genesis 12:2, *"I will bless you…and you shall be a blessing."*

God has prepared a place of favor and blessing for you—a place of safety and power. As you *"seek first the kingdom of God and His righteousness,"* remember that, *"all these things shall be added to you"* (Matt. 6:33). I encourage you to press into the Spirit and expectantly pursue your place of authority—to seek out your place in the Kingdom. Your journey to your seat of authority starts by looking within. It is a place of authority you step into "in the spirit"—within your own heart, mind, and soul—*"For indeed, the kingdom of God is within you"* (Luke 17:21). As you align your innermost intentions with God's eternal purposes, get in position to receive and to be God's blessing in the earth.

> *Return to the stronghold, you prisoners of hope. Even today I declare that I will restore double to you. ... "So I will strengthen them in the Lord, and they shall walk up and down in His name," says the Lord* (Zechariah 9:12; 10:12).

## GETTING IN POSITION

There is a connection between living by faith and being blessed. One of the keys to walking in God's blessing is having the faith of "believing Abraham"—a faith that simply believes God.

- When has God directed you to head in

a completely foreign direction? Were you able to step out in faith and trust Him?

- How is your ability to trust God connected to your capacity to obey Him?
- How can you know you are in the right place and that it is truly the blessing of the Lord chasing you?

# CHAPTER 4

# THE PLUMB LINE PRINCIPLE

*Then He showed me another vision. I saw
the Lord standing beside a wall that had
been built using a plumb line. He was using
a plumb line to see if it was still straight.
And the Lord said to me, "Amos, what do
you see?" I answered, "A plumb line." And
the Lord replied, "I will test My people with
this plumb line. I will no longer ignore all
their sins. The pagan shrines of your ances-
tors will be ruined, and the temples of
Israel will be destroyed; I will bring the
dynasty of King Jeroboam to a sudden end."*
(Amos 7:7-9 NLT)

Israel was prospering at the time Amos was shown this
vision of the plumb line. Under King Jeroboam, Israel had

developed into a wealthy nation and Jerusalem was its affluent capital. Surrounded by flourishing cities, beautiful palaces, and strong armies, the Israelites had grown comfortable in a false sense of stability and safety. God's chosen people had become lazy and self-indulgent. They had grown accustomed to their cozy lifestyles, were increasingly distracted by worldly pleasures, and grew ever more complacent toward their God. Listen to how they are portrayed in Amos 6:4-6 (NLT):

> *How terrible for you who sprawl on ivory beds and lounge on your couches, eating the meat of tender lambs from the flock and of choice calves fattened in the stall. You sing trivial songs to the sound of the harp and fancy yourselves to be great musicians like David. You drink wine by the bowlful and perfume yourselves with fragrant lotions. You care nothing about the ruin of your nation.*

God was extremely displeased with Israel. God's prophet, Amos, after being given two other visions depicting God's judgment upon the people, steps in on their behalf. He pleads with God to show mercy. He intercedes for the nation, and God agrees to hold back His wrath on one condition: They come into alignment; they line up with His Word of righteousness. God gives Amos a vision of the plumb line to illustrate His point.

Notice that in this vision the Lord is standing next to a wall that is already built "to plumb"—or built straight by using a plumb line. The standard has already been set. The common instrument used to check its alignment is probably the most ancient measuring device known to masons, bricklayers, and builders of all kinds. It was a plumb line that gauged the symmetry of the Egyptian pyramids, the alignment of the Greek temples, and the proportions of the Roman basilicas—the world's greatest structures—and they are still standing today.

But unless you've worked in construction, masonry, or carpentry, you're probably not familiar with the concept of the plumb line. For centuries, when builders would construct cathedrals, for example, they would mark the center of the floor, and as they built the ceiling higher and higher, they would suspend a plumb line from it to make sure the center—or apex—of the ceiling aligned with the mark on the floor. This ensured the dome of the cathedral was symmetrical and would not collapse. It gave the structure durability so that when storms and winds and natural disasters took place, the building would be secure at its strongest point: its center.

In medical terms, the plumb line is defined as "an undeviating vertical line that serves as a reference when evaluating postural alignment."[1] This is a great definition to help us describe the spiritual plumb line used on the Body of Christ. God uses His plumb line to describe what He is doing as He builds His living temple, and how He is bringing His Body—the Church in the earth today—into alignment with His Word and His will.

## PLUMB LINE SEASON

*Behold, I am setting a plumb line as a standard in the midst of My people* (Amos 7:8 AMP).

Today in the Body of Christ, we are entering a season when God is holding up a plumb line, much like He did during the reign of King Jeroboam. He has established His Word as the standard with which His Church must align. It is no surprise that during a time of unprecedented wealth and prosperity, as we languish on our couches indulging ourselves with every sort of pleasure, that God would drop a plumb line amongst His people just as He did in the time of Amos.

Even as the Lord told Amos, *"I will test My people with this plumb line,"* so the Spirit of God is testing His people today. If we pay attention, we will recognize God's plumb lines being set forth. We will hear the word "plumb line" used more commonly throughout the Church across the nations. This is a season of testing and alignment. Why? Why is God dropping a plumb line in this era? I believe we are moving into a season where there is no pre-established blueprint for what God is about to do. We must be open to an entirely new plan.

So how can we know what the new blueprint is, or if it is of God? We must begin by discerning the plumb lines God is dropping among His people—His Church—His Temple. It is the tool God is using in this late hour to ensure that His Living Temple is being built to the correct standard. God is actively preparing His Bride to be revealed in all her glory. And don't think that because you are not a pastor or in full-time ministry God is not speaking to you as part of this move. This not only applies to the Body of Christ corporately, but to each of you individually. In the same way He is calling His Church to align with His Word, He is calling you as an individual to fall in line with His will.

Now the good news for those of us living under the New Covenant is that the ultimate plumb line has already been made manifest in Jesus Christ. Christ is our

> *I believe we are moving into a season where there is no pre-established blueprint for what God is about to do. We must be open to an entirely new plan.*

standard of measurement; He is the *living* plumb line. Not only that, He is the chief cornerstone against which every living stone—each one of us—must be aligned. God in His mercy has given us His Word, His Spirit, and the power of His name to equip and empower us to do just that.

## BUILT TO LAST

*Unless the Lord builds the house, they labor in vain who build it; unless the Lord guards the city, the watchman stays awake in vain* (Psalm 127:1).

God's original DNA—His original blueprint for what you're building in your life—is meant to survive through time, through circumstances, through spiritual warfare, through things you see, and through things you don't see. The building of God—that's *you*—is meant to stand. That's why He says, "*On this rock I will build My church, and the gates of Hades shall not prevail against it*" (Matt. 16:18). Your life in Christ, built on the rock of His Word, is designed to not only withstand all the powers of hell, but also to crash through its gates. Listen to how The Message states it: "*I will put together My church, a church so expansive with energy that not even the gates of hell will be able to keep it out.*" Now that's powerful!

But look now at Matthew 7:21 (NLT). Jesus is teaching a series of powerful parables and gives this warning to His listeners: "Not everyone who calls out to Me, 'Lord! Lord!' will enter the Kingdom of Heaven. Only those who actually do the will of My Father in heaven will enter." There is a condition you must fulfill that goes beyond simply calling Jesus "Lord." The Bible says even demons believe and tremble. Jesus goes on to explain: "On judgment day many will say to Me, 'Lord! Lord! We prophesied in Your name and cast out demons in Your name and performed many miracles in Your name.' But I will reply, 'I never knew you. Get away from Me, you who break God's laws'" (Matt. 7:22-23 NLT). You must not only hear God's voice to be saved, but you must also obey it.

> *God's original DNA—His original blueprint for what you're building in your life—is meant to survive through time, through circumstances, through spiritual warfare, through things you see, and through things you don't see.*

Now let's get back to building our life to stand while we are alive in the earth. Jesus is making it plain (for those of us who are a little slow) about how exactly we are to construct our lives to stand firm against any enemy onslaught. Look at the next four verses:

*Anyone who listens to My teaching and follows it is wise, like a person who builds a house on solid rock. Though the rain comes in torrents and the floodwaters rise and the winds beat against that house, it won't collapse because it is built on bedrock. But anyone who hears My teaching and doesn't obey it is foolish, like a person who builds a house on sand. When the rains and floods come and the winds beat against that house, it will collapse with a mighty crash* (Matthew 7:24-27 NLT).

Jesus isn't saying that all who listen to His teaching will stand strong against adversity. No, He is telling us that only those who listen and then *do* what He says will remain strong. His purpose is for you to build your life upon the rock of His Word and stand. That is why in Matthew 16:18 He said, *"On this rock I will build My church."* His Church is a living organism made up of living stones. You and I are the living stones He uses to construct His house— His habitation here on the earth. Now He didn't say "living bricks," did He? God's building is not made of bricks because

> *You must not only hear God's voice to be saved, but you must also obey it.*

bricks are exactly uniform—each exactly the same. You are not a living *brick;* you are a living *stone* because you've been specially carved out to fit precisely in the unique place prepared for you. You have not been factory formed and then half-baked; you have been hewn to order.

There is a stonemason who lives in Martha's Vineyard who constructs amazing works of art with rocks. He painstakingly compiles hand-chosen stones to build what some consider architectural feats—archways, multi-story fireplaces, even entire cottages—from individual rocks he simply fits together in remarkable ways. A reporter's observations reminded me of what Christ does with each of us: "As usual, he has assembled thousands of stones to choose from. As usual, he has handpicked every one. And, as usual, without chiseling or altering the face of the stone in any way, he will make sure they all fit perfectly, no matter how long it takes."

Imagine how much more difficult it is to build a house out of different shapes and sizes of stone compared to bricks. Bricks can easily be laid in neat rows because they are all exactly the same. However, as living stones, not only do we come in infinite varieties of textures, colors, shapes, and sizes, but we are constantly changing. It's one thing to take a stationary slab of stone and position it, while it's quite another to build a structure from individual living stones that are moving and breathing and growing, each with its own will.

But God is up for the challenge. He is constructing His sanctuary out of living stones that have a mind and will of their own. This is why He must drop a plumb line into the building of His Church—so He can show whether it is being built in alignment with Heaven. In Matthew 7:26 Jesus is illustrating this concept. He is saying that His teaching is the plumb line, and that those who hear it and do not line up their life with it are like fools who build their lives upon shifting sands of uncertainty. When the storms come, that which they have built *"will collapse with a mighty crash."* Like in our cathedral example earlier, if the dome is not erected perfectly plumb, it will collapse at the first test of bad weather.

> *You must align everything in your life according to the plumb line of Heaven: the Bible.*

Usually you don't know a house isn't built to plumb until disaster strikes. The exterior might look beautiful and sturdy, but once the high winds blow, or the water rises, or the ground shakes, the foundation cracks and the roof caves in. Until there is stress placed upon the structure, you cannot know its true condition or strength. This is why you must be sure that as you build your life, your family, your ministry, and your business, that you build according to God's plumb line—according to the truth of His Word. You must align everything in your life according to the plumb line of Heaven: the Bible.

This is how God brings alignment into your life—and therefore victory, blessing, and success.

## BRINGING IT HOME

*For the time has come for judgment to begin at the house of God; and if it begins with us first, what will be the end of those who do not obey the gospel of God?* (1 Peter 4:17)

In the vision where God showed Amos about the plumb line, the Lord is standing by a wall that is already built to plumb. If we were to make that applicable to us today, we could say that the wall God is standing beside represents His Word that is forever settled in Heaven. Any plumb line on earth is always patterned after something that is settled in Heaven. The Bible says that although the Word of God is settled in Heaven, it must be established on earth. Jesus taught us to pray, *"Your kingdom come. Your will be done on earth as it is in heaven"* (Matt. 6:10). When we speak of "establishing God's Word," we are talking about knowing, praying, and speaking God's Word;

we are talking about the knowledge of God's Word governing all that we do. This is important because the Word of God is powerful, alive, and eternal. (See Hebrews 4:12.) Jesus said that Heaven and earth will pass away, but His Word will never pass away. (See Matthew 24:35.)

In Hebrews 12:25-27 we are told that as God once shook the earth with His voice, He will shake it again. God shook the mountain where He met with Moses; but when God shakes the earth again, He will also shake the heavens: *"Yet once more I shake not only the earth, but also heaven"* (Heb. 12:26). The writer goes on to explain the reason for this second shaking: *"'Yet once more,' indicates the removal of those things that are being shaken, as of things that are made, that the things which cannot be shaken may remain"* (Heb. 12:27). We are being told here in the New Testament that a major shaking is coming. This shaking will cause everything that is not aligned with God's Word to fall. Everything will be shaken—the heavens and the earth—but only that which is born of the eternal Word of God will remain.

The good news is that in God's loving mercy He always brings fair warning to His people. There will be opportunity to align what you're doing with what God is about to do—or else, according to the Scripture, great will be the fall of it. You will not, however, be caught unaware. You will not be ignorant of what is taking place on the earth. Here you are now, reading this book! I'm telling you, through these pages God will speak into your life whatever it is you need to know, if you will listen to what the Spirit is saying. But it is up to you to follow His voice—just as Jesus taught in Matthew 7. If you listen to His voice and do what He tells you, when the shaking comes, your house will stand.

A shaking is coming. God's plumb line has dropped. There will be judgment on the earth, and it will begin with the Church. Judgment will start within the Body of Christ because God is most concerned about His own people; His covenant is with the New Testament Church, not the nations of the world.

> *God will speak into your life whatever it is you need to know, if you will listen to what the Spirit is saying.*

God is aligning *His* House—He is preparing *His* Body—for the great thing He is about to do. Therefore, the House of God is also the staging ground for everything God is wanting to do on the earth. God is dropping a plumb line in the midst of the Church in order to showcase His righteousness.

Look at First Peter 4:17 again: "For the time has come for judgment to begin at the house of God; and if it begins with us first, what will be the end of those who do not obey the gospel of God?" There is hope for those of us in God's own house. "For the Lord disciplines the one He loves, and chastises every son whom He receives" (Heb. 12:6 ESV). God disciplines those He loves so He can lead them to places of greater victory and blessing. He doesn't automatically transport them there after He chastises them, however; He leads them through each lesson step by step. God, like the good Father He is, painstakingly trains His children to make better choices.

God disciplines those He loves so they can make smarter decisions. The word *judgment* that Peter uses here in First Peter 4:17 is the Greek word *krema*—a type of judgment that can be affected by the power of decision. In other words, when judgment begins in this sense, you will have opportunity beforehand to make a choice. God's judgment is not going to catch you off guard. Peter is saying that judgment will begin in God's House because we are the people tuned into His voice. We will hear what God is saying and have an opportunity to make adjustments. The word *krema* denotes that there will be an opportunity to choose, to decide, to align with His judgment—and our decisions

> *God, like the good Father He is, painstakingly trains His children to make better choices.*

will be the first measured against Heaven's plumb line.

God is putting His house in order; and for Him to order His Church, He must first bring order into every believer's private home. He is looking for the fruit of righteousness to be revealed in the lives of His people, as we conduct our daily affairs at home and in the workplace. This is the Church that the world sees. Make sure they see a Church built on the rock.

## A PROPER ORDER

*And David said to all the assembly of Israel, "If it seems good to you, and if it is of the Lord our God, let us... bring the ark of our God back to us, for we have not inquired at it since the days of Saul." Then all the assembly said that they would do so, for the thing was right in the eyes of all the people* (1 Chronicles 13:2-4).

In First Chronicles 13, we read about David inquiring of the assembly if he should bring the Ark of the Covenant back to Israel. David thought it would be good to bring the glory and the presence of God back into the midst of His people. The entire assembly agreed that this would be the right thing to do, and so David and his men set out with the Ark. *"They carried the ark of God on a new cart from the house of Abinadab, and Uzza and Ahio drove the cart"* (1 Chron. 13:7). David and the Israelites followed along, celebrating with all of their might before God, *"with singing, on harps, on stringed instruments, on tambourines, on cymbals, and with trumpets"* (1 Chron. 13:8). They were praising and worshiping God. They were rejoicing that the glory of God would be coming to their city.

How many people in the Body of Christ today are hungry for His glory? How many have prayed for revival or made great sacrifices to see the glory of God manifested? We are now moving into an era where we will see more of the glory of God. It is for this reason that God is asking us to measure ourselves according to His plumb line—because when the glory comes and things are not to plumb, the glory will not only bring life, but also judgment. When the weightiness and the majesty of God descends into a place that is chaotic and out of order, it will be swallowed up and destroyed by the impact of God's glory. Alignment must always precede the glory of the Lord.

This is why God sets a plumb line among His people, so the glory of God can bring blessing and not judgment. God does not want His Church to be ignorant. Look what happens in First Chronicles 13:9-10. The oxen that are pulling the cart carrying the Ark of the Covenant stumbled. Uzza put out his hand to steady the Ark and aroused the anger of the Lord. The Lord *"struck him because he put his hand to the ark; and he died there before God."* In the next verse we read that David became angry, and then frightened, because the Lord's wrath had broken out against Uzza. We are told that to this day this place is called *Perez Uzza*, which means the "breaking forth of God on Uzza."

David was nervous. He was afraid to move the Ark any farther. Here he is, the nation's king, prophet, and priest—his heart hungry for more of God, desperate for God's presence—and he knows he needs the Ark nearby to be near God's glory. David is doing the best he knows how. He is leading the people in worship, and they are praising God and bringing the Lord honor and glory even as they carefully transport the Ark. No doubt their motives are right, just as Uzza's were as he reached out to steady the Ark. Yet he was struck dead! What happened? Uzza hit a plumb line in the Spirit! Although his heart was right, he was not following God's blueprint. In the same way, many today are trying to build God's house

> *When the weightiness and the majesty of God descends into a place that is chaotic and out of order, it will be swallowed up and destroyed by the impact of God's glory.*

according to their own understanding, not according to God's design, and they are heading for disaster because of it. They are not building it true to plumb, and great will be the fall of it!

First Chronicles 15:13 puts it this way: *"The Lord our God broke out against us, because we did not consult Him about the proper order."* It's one thing to seek God, but it's another thing to seek Him according to His divine order. In this particular incident they did not seek God about the proper order. They hit an invisible plumb line— which is prophetically symbolic in our day of what will happen to ministries if they are not built according to God's specs.

Uzza hit God's holy plumb line, and it took him out. The Israelites had lost their grasp on some basic facts, including the hazards of handling the Ark of the Covenant outside of the Levitical Order of the Priest-hood. In the Old Testament, there was a due order set in motion that would allow the priests to handle the Ark. A few verses later we learn that they take the Ark and put it at Obed Edom's house, and Obed Edom gets blessed. He gets blessed while Uzza drops dead. Why? Because Obed Edom was a Levitical porter who was an assigned gate-keeper of the Ark. So while the Ark remained in his juris-diction, it blessed him.

David finally goes back for the Ark, but this time he

brings the Levites. The priests know exactly what to do because they have found God's blueprint—God's pattern for carrying the glory. They followed God's outline and successfully brought the Ark back to Israel. We too must learn to correctly usher God's glory back into the house of God. It's OK to want the glory and be passionate about God, but we must be circumspect.

Too often we take God's Spirit, His presence, and His glory for granted. Be careful! This is why inexplicable things happen in people's lives. If you conduct yourself according to your own personal plumb line without taking into consideration God's pattern—His proper order—then some of you could end up like Uzza!

> *It's OK to want the glory and be passionate about God, but we must be circumspect.*

## THE FEAR FACTOR

*The Spirit that gives direction and builds strength, the Spirit that instills knowledge and Fear-of-God. Fear-of-God will be all his joy and delight.... Each morning he'll pull on sturdy work clothes and boots, and*

*build righteousness and faithfulness in the
land* (Isaiah 11:1-5 TM).

How will you know when a plumb has been dropped into the midst of your life? You will know you've come up against God's plumb line because it will instill a holy fear of God. A godly fear will come forth and you will experience a fresh awareness of His majesty and holiness. You will be so aware of God that a sacred awe and reverence will grip you so that you won't want to mess anything up. Little things that need your attention will pop out; things you never paid attention to before will suddenly seem very important. You will be acutely aware of every word that comes out of your mouth and every thought that crosses your mind. This is how you will know God is setting His plumb line.

In Acts 5, under the ministry of Peter the apostle, a great move of God was taking place. Three thousand people came to the Lord in one day. God added to the Church daily; there was a tremendous unity among the brethren, and signs and wonders were common. The Holy Spirit was moving with power. People were moved to give all their wealth to the work of the ministry; they sold their property, their homes, and all their belongings to give into the Church.

But then we have Ananias and Sapphira. These folks

decide that they're going to hold something back for themselves. They sold their property, committing to give all the proceeds to the ministry. When the time came to hand over their offering, however, they lied. They attempted to deceive the apostles, and in doing so, they lied to God. Peter summoned Ananias and confronted him with the evil of his deed. He asked him why he allowed satan to fill his heart to lie to the Holy Spirit. *"Why have you conceived this thing in your heart? You have not lied to men but to God"* (Acts 5:4). At this, Ananias drops dead.

When people are walking out of alignment and they encounter the glory of God, it will knock them out. And I'm not talking about being slain in the Spirit, I'm talking about being slain *period.* I'm telling you that while there will be people raised from the dead in this era, there will also be some who will drop dead. We cannot mess with the glory of God—and God's glory is coming! When God's plumb line drops down and you run up against it, if your life is not plumb, it will take you out! This is why you have to make sure you're plumb for what God is about to do.

Look at what happens to Ananias' wife, Sapphira. Peter calls her in after they take her dead husband out the door and asks her if she and her husband turned in the full price from the sale of their property. She lies and tells him, "Yes."

Then Peter said to her, *"How is it that you have agreed together to test the Spirit of the Lord? Look, the feet of those who have buried your husband are at the door, and they will carry you out"* (Acts 5:9). She too immediately fell down and died, *"And the young men came in and found her dead, and carrying her out, buried her by her husband"* (Acts 5:10). They had a burial ministry. We don't have that in our usher manuals today: "What to do when folks drop dead on Sunday morning for lying about an offering to the Lord." It is something to think about.

> *The fear of God and the comfort of the Spirit go together; they are both important to understanding God's plumb line.*

More importantly, however, there was spiritual fruit that began to abound in the Church as a result. That fruit was the fear of God. *"So great fear came upon all the church and upon all who heard these things"* (Acts 5:11). Why is the fear of God important? The fear of God will keep you from the pit. The comfort of the Holy Spirit will get you out once you are there, but it is the fear of God that will keep you from falling into it.

The fear of God and the comfort of the Spirit go together; they are both important to understanding God's plumb line. You will undoubtedly make mistakes, but if you repent, God will forgive you and His Spirit will comfort you. It is also important to understand how to walk in the fear of God in order to avoid the pits and traps that can pull you off course and set you back. It is better to build correctly the first time than continually reconstruct and repair what you have done.

## FIREPROOFING

*Now if anyone builds on the foundation with gold, silver, precious stones, wood, hay, straw—each one's work will become manifest, for the Day will disclose it, because it will be revealed by fire, and the fire will test what sort of work each one has done. If the work that anyone has built on the foundation survives, he will receive a reward* (1 Corinthians 3:12-14 ESV).

Our building—our work—must be sound. It will have to withstand some tests. We read in First Corinthians 3:13 (KJV) that, *"Every man's work shall be made manifest,"* because it will ultimately be *"revealed by fire."* A day will come when the fire of God will try every man's work to determine the quality of it in eternal terms—in other words, whether a person's work lines up with the eternal purposes of God or not. I want you to notice the verse here is talking about an individual's *work*—not about the individual. The Scripture is saying that every work will be tried by fire, not every man. We are then told that if any man's work survives, meaning if it withstands the fire, he shall receive a reward.

So how do you fireproof your work? God has set forth His plumb line for this very reason. You are able to gauge the eternal durability of your work by using this holy measuring system. This is the same system God will use when He evaluates your work. He has given you the ability now to do the "pre-testing." God is saying to the Body of Christ today that every ministry and business, every great vision and divine assignment, every call that God has given His men and women, will have to pass the fire test. And He has provided the equipment necessary to do the fireproofing.

You, however, are always more valuable than what you build. God is interested in what you are building simply because it is a product of who you are. What you become is more important than what you build. The building process is what gives you opportunity to learn, grow, and change *"from glory to glory"* (see 2 Cor. 3:18). God is not interested in your building because He knows that unless *He* builds the house, *"...they labor in vain who build it"* (Ps. 127:1). He's not asking you to build; He's saying, "I'll build My house! I'll build My Church! I'll do the building, but I also want to do the changing in you first." And changing you precedes building. Because ultimately, what you build is an expression of who you are.

If you don't deal with who you are before doing anything else, your identity will become wrapped up in what you build—you won't be able to separate who you are from what you do—and when the fire comes, your identity will be burnt up with the vain thing you've built. You won't know who you are because what you've built will define you. Make sure you are able to distinguish your role from the Lord's, your work from the Lord's work, and who it is you are in Christ.

> *What you become is more important than what you build.*

## BUILD ON THE ROCK

*Let each one take heed how he builds.... For no other foundation can anyone lay than that which is laid, which is Jesus Christ* (1 Corinthians 3:10-11).

Although we are entering a new era and a new work is being built, the foundation always remains the same.

The rock upon which we build never changes. The architecture may look different, but the support structure is constant. There is but one measurement to which all things must be aligned; there is but one solid rock. Listen to what God is saying and apply His Word to every decision you make. Walk in that light no matter how hard it is, and don't compromise. It's the little compromises that throw you off plumb.

Compromising is different from making a mistake. Compromising is intentionally choosing to act contrary to God's Word. In that *krema* moment you are given the chance to judge yourself, and if you choose not to, it is a subtle, yet willful, disobedience. On the other hand, you will inevitably make mistakes; that is how you learn and grow. It is what you do with those mistakes that matter. If you are quick to acknowledge when you've missed it and make adjustments, you'll find that you are building a solid work, true to plumb.

Let me tell you something about breaking through to a new level. Often you feel you are ready to push on through, not realizing that God's hand is keeping you where you are in order to protect you. God will put a ceiling on your promotion because your life isn't aligned exactly right. This is the time to take a good look within yourself, while at the same time discerning what is going on around you. You may think it is the devil holding you back, so you're doing everything possible to rebuke him, but really it is God saying that you are not ready. You're not fighting the devil; you're fighting God's own hand. The apostle Paul did this very thing. Jesus had to stop him in the middle of the road and ask, *"Why are you persecuting Me?"* Paul thought he was doing God a service, but he was actually fighting against Him. (See Acts 26:14.)

The ceiling you bump up against in your life could be a type of plumb line representing God's attempt to recalibrate you so that you are a *"vessel for honor, sanctified and useful for the Master, prepared for every good work"* (2 Tim. 2:21). If you are not prepared, you are not protected. God will protect you by keeping you from going somewhere you're not ready to go. God wants you to get your life in order so that

> *If you are quick to acknowledge when you've missed it and make adjustments, you'll find that you are building a solid work, true to plumb.*

you will be able to withstand whatever comes against you. The higher you go, the greater the opposition. God knows that if your life is not built according to plumb, you will be destroyed. To hold holy things, a vessel must first be sanctified. This is what God is doing throughout the Body of Christ; He is preparing His Body to go to another level. He is preparing His vessels to hold greater, more powerful things.

God is giving you the opportunity to make some choices—to judge (*krema*) yourself—to decide how you are going to move forward. These are not one-time decisions that you make on Sunday morning at the altar; these are daily decisions about how you are going to live. You must be brave enough to ask, "Lord, where's the plumb line? Show me the plumb line, and let's make sure I've built everything according to plumb." God is pleased with that; He will help you in those areas. After all, that is why He drops the plumb line, to help you.

> *These are not one-time decisions that you make on Sunday morning at the altar; these are daily decisions about how you are going to live.*

Many people are called in this era to do things that have never been done before. There are callings, giftings, and anointings in the earth today such as the world has never seen. More importantly, however, God does not want you to lose your identity in the process of building your ministry. Don't build on your gift; build on the rock, which is the revelation of God's Word. That's why Jesus said to Peter in Matthew 16:17-18, *"For flesh and blood has not revealed this to you, but My Father who is in heaven...and on this rock I will build My church, and the gates of Hades shall not prevail against it."*

You are God's building. Make sure your foundation is built on Christ. When you do that, whatever you build will stand against every storm in the earth, every enemy in hell, and every fire from Heaven. Build with an eternal perspective according to Heaven's eternal plumb line: the eternal Word of God.

> *Forever, O Lord, Your word is settled in heaven. Your faithfulness endures to all generations; You established the earth, and it abides. They continue this day according to Your ordinances, for all are Your servants. Unless Your law had been my delight, I would then have perished in my affliction. I will never forget Your precepts, for by them You have given me life. I am Yours, save me; for I have sought Your precepts* (Psalm 119:89-94).

## ⚜ GETTING IN POSITION ⚜

Christ is your standard of measurement—He is the living plumb line. God has given you His Word, His Spirit, and the power of His Name to equip and empower you to get into alignment.

- How have you used the tools you've been given?

God disciplines those He loves so He can lead them to places of greater victory and blessing. God painstakingly trains His children to make better choices.

- How have you felt the Lord disciplining you?
- How has God's "training" brought blessing to your life?

God is asking us to measure ourselves according to His plumb line—because when the glory comes and things are not to plumb, the glory will not only bring life, but it will also judge.

- Have you sensed there are some little things that might need adjusting?
- Pray and listen to hear if God brings something to your attention.

### ENDNOTES

1. Ann Asher, "Plumb Line," http://backandneck .about.com/od/p/g/plumb.htm (accessed December 9, 2007).

2. Steve Hartman, "Lew French, The Rock Master," *CBS News* (November 11, 2007).

CHAPTER 5

# THE PATH TO PROMISE

*Then Jesus was led up by the Spirit into*
*the wilderness to be tempted by the devil*
(Matthew 4:1).

Not a single great prophet, leader, or king portrayed in the Bible managed to bypass the wilderness. In fact, the greater God's anointing, the dryer the desert, the deeper the pit, and the darker the cave. Think about the patriarchs and how God sent them *all* into a season of hardship. God tested the faith of Abraham, Jacob, Joseph, and Moses. Joseph spent 14 years in prison before he rose to the right hand of Pharaoh from where he ushered the children of Israel into Egypt. Moses spent 40 years on the backside of the desert before God used him to lead the children of Israel out of Egypt. And on their way to the Promised Land, where did God lead the newly liberated Israelites? Straight into the wilderness!

The path to promise always leads through the wilderness. Think about the mighty David who suffered years of exile as a fugitive from the wrath of King Saul. We find David—a man after God's own heart—hiding out in a remote cave, as did Elijah, before becoming one of the Bible's greatest leaders and prophets. With the dawning of the New Covenant, we are introduced to Jesus, the most anointed of all. Jesus, who is the *Christ*—"God's Anointed"—spends 40 days without food *in the desert*— alone, that is, except for His tempter, satan.

> *The path to promise always leads through the wilderness.*

Through the experience of Christ, we are given tremendous insight into what God is doing when He leads those He loves into the wilderness. Here we see Jesus, God's own beloved Son in whom He is well pleased, *"full of the Holy Spirit,"* having just been baptized in the Jordan River so that all righteousness may be fulfilled. (See Matthew 3:15-17 and Luke 4:1-2.) At the conclusion of this momentous occasion, the heavens open up, the

Spirit of God descends, and a loud voice is heard to say, *"This is My beloved Son...."* After all of that fanfare, Jesus is led away into the desert to starve and be harassed by the devil. What kind of a promotion, let alone celebration, is that?

Is this what we should all expect after an encounter with God? There are many of you who have received a word from the Father. Perhaps the heavens didn't open up, but the Lord has spoken to you, called you His beloved, and His Spirit has alighted upon you. Many of you have received a word from God, but your life has never changed. You have felt God release you to set sail, but you remain moored at the dock—stuck in a particular phase of your life. I believe there are insights you can learn from Jesus' wilderness experience that will help you transition from where you are now to where it is God would have you go.

## THE WILDERNESS TESTS

*And suddenly a voice came from heaven, saying, "This is My beloved Son, in whom I am well pleased"* (Matthew 3:17).

When the Father speaks, He has one thing in mind: revealing His Son. Jesus had been waiting all of His life to hear God say these particular words. He knew He had a call on His life; He had been about His Father's business since the age of 12. Yet Jesus did not step out until He heard God speak forth this word concerning Him. And what was that defining word? *"This is My beloved Son, in whom I am well pleased."* He had waited until He was 30 years old for His Father to reveal His identity and release Him into His destiny as God's beloved Son.

The next few verses tell us what happened right after this word from God was spoken over Jesus:

> *Then Jesus was led up by the Spirit into the wilderness to be tempted by the devil. And when He had fasted forty days and forty nights, afterward He was hungry. Now when the tempter came to Him, he said, "If You are the Son of God, command that these stones become bread." But He answered and said, "It is written, 'Man shall not live by bread alone, but by every word that proceeds from the mouth of God'"* (Matthew 4:1-4).

As soon as the Word concerning Him proceeds from the mouth of God, Jesus sets off to fulfill His divine assignment—His eternal purpose. He embarks on this epic journey by heading straight into the wilderness. Here we have Jesus, upon whom the Spirit of God has just descended; He has just been baptized, filled with the Holy Spirit, and called out by God. And now that same loving Father leads Him directly into the wilderness to be tempted by the devil. Mark 1:12 states: *"Immediately the Spirit drove Him into the wilderness."* If this had happened to you or I, we would have thought we'd missed it somewhere—that we hadn't heard God correctly. We certainly would not expect to be driven into the wilderness by the Holy Spirit for the express purpose of being tempted by satan!

Yet this is the itinerary God had planned for Jesus. His path to promise led straight into the wilderness. He headed for the desert, deprived Himself of food and water, contended with wild beasts, and waited for the enemy to show up. After 40 days, when Jesus was at His weakest point, the devil took his best shot. Jesus must have been thinking about His empty stomach when the devil put forth his challenge, *"If you are the Son of God, command that these stones become bread"* (Matt. 4:3). Jesus gave the life-defining, Heaven-aligning response that the universe had stood poised to hear since the beginning of time: Jesus answers and says, *"It is written, 'Man shall not live by bread alone, but by every word that proceeds from the mouth of God'"* (Matt. 4:4).

That was the answer that won Jesus His eternal prize: His seat of authority at the right hand of the Father. In that moment of decision, that *krema* moment, Jesus chooses to align Himself with the written Word of God. We see the plumb line principle in effect as Jesus faced His first test in the wilderness. We know He suffered the same temptations as you or I would, for we are told in Hebrews 4:15 that He *"was in all points tempted as we are"* and in Hebrews 2:18 that, *"He Himself has suffered, being tempted."* In that moment, Jesus made a decision—He made a judgment—to live *"by every word that proceeds from the mouth of God,"* and nothing else.

> *The first key is to understand exactly what it means to live* "by every word that proceeds from the mouth of God."

This was just the first of three temptations—or tests—that Jesus would encounter. He passes them all with flying colors. But there are some significant keys you can learn from studying each encounter in more depth that will help you pass these very same tests along your own path to promise. The first key is to understand exactly what it means to live *"by every word that proceeds from the mouth of God."* To do that, you will need to look at where this decree was originally written.

In Deuteronomy chapter 8, God is speaking to the people of Israel. They had escaped Egypt, passed through the Red Sea, and found themselves in a barren wilderness where they wandered in circles for the next 40 years. In Deuteronomy 8:2 God gives the reason, *"You shall remember that the Lord your God led you all the way these forty years in the wilderness, to humble you and test you, to know what was in your heart, whether you would keep His commandments or not."*

There was something about the wilderness that challenged every fiber of their being. At one point they said they would rather return to the bondage of their former masters than remain in the wilderness and face the openness of their hearts before the presence of God. What was it about the wilderness that compelled them to so resist this—to want to return to bondage and grumble against the God who had at last set them free? How could they choose laboring in the brickyards of Egypt for cruel masters over a scenic road trip with their heavenly Father? This is what God wants to have some of you find out about your life.

But there's more. The next verse tells us what is at the core of all this humbling and testing: *"He humbled you, allowed you to hunger, and fed you with manna which you did not know nor did your fathers know, that **He might make you know that man shall not live by bread alone;***

*but man lives by every word that proceeds from the mouth of the Lord"* (Deut. 8:3). The bottom line is the knowledge that you do not live by what you create with your hands, but what God creates through His Word, *"that the universe was created by the word of God"* (Heb. 11:3 ESV), and *"The Word gave life to everything that was created"* (John 1:4 NLT).

The purpose for humbling you is not to humiliate you or force you to submit to some legalistic system, or even to suffer a while so that you can "overcome the flesh." It doesn't have anything to do with learning discipline and controlling your carnal desires. It is simply about learning to trust God. He is saying that He leads you into the wilderness so that He can get you to that intimate place of humility before Him—where He can strip you of all your fashionable clothes, your socially acceptable manners and politically correct viewpoints—that quiet place where He can whisper in your ear and speak truth into your life. He wants to dismantle every bondage and addiction holding you captive and free you from every constraint, even if it requires that you go hungry for a time. God will do whatever it takes to

> *you do not live by what you create with your hands, but what God creates through His Word...*

bring you to taste of the authentic nourishment of His Word and make clear the true source of your provision.

Until you are in a place of need, or faced with your own crisis of conviction, you will never be fully convinced of spiritual truth. The tests you encounter in the wilderness are the tools God uses to establish your faith—to personally demonstrate to you that your life is not sustained by the temporal world that you can see, but by the unseen, eternal Word of Truth. That this Truth would become a reality in the depths of your heart is the primary reason why the Spirit of God leads you—or drives you— into the wilderness. The first challenge posed to you in the wilderness is, "On what do you base your faith?" Are you going to rely on natural resources, represented by bread, or are you going to rely on the life-sustaining Word of God?" This is what I call the "Bread Test."

> *It is simply about learning to trust God.*

## The Bread Test

> *Show me Your ways, O Lord; teach me Your paths. Lead me in Your truth and teach me, for You are the God of my salvation; on*

*You I wait all the day. ... Good and upright is the Lord; therefore He teaches sinners in the way. The humble He guides in justice, and the humble He teaches His way* (Psalm 25:4-5,8-9).

David understood that the Lord shows His ways to the humble and meek. If you are to succeed, you must know God's ways, and if you are to know them, you must humble yourself before the mighty hand of God. First Peter 5:5 reminds us that, *"God resists the proud, but gives grace to the humble."* Micah asks, *"What does the Lord require of you but...to walk humbly with your God?"* (Mic. 6:8). In the Book of Daniel, we read, *"from the first day that you set your heart to understand, and to humble yourself before your God, your words were heard"* (Dan. 10:12). The first step to understanding the central truth of the Bread Test—that man *"lives by every word that proceeds from the mouth of God"*—is to humble ourselves.

When you find yourself in the wilderness, don't harden your heart, but soften it. Don't get bitter or frustrated, but open your heart to receive the word of God. There is no other way to pass this first critical test. There is no other ticket out of the wilderness. You can quote Scripture all day long, you can go to meetings and services every day of the week, but until you become familiar with the ways of God you will continue to circle the wilderness. It doesn't matter how many years you have been in business, how many miles you've traveled in the ministry, or even whether you are doing what God has called you to do—you can still be stuck. You can be stuck in different places of the wilderness at the same time; you can be in a dry wasteland regarding your business, lost in the woods with your ministry, and in a dark cave when it comes to your family. Where do you need to humble yourself so that you can line up and walk in the truth?

I know what it's like to be stuck in the wilderness. I've made a few extra trips back to some barren places in my life and feel like I am familiar with every nook and cranny of every rocky slope along the way. There are streets named after me in the wilderness. Maybe you feel the same. Perhaps you've been around the same old mountain and have seen the same stones along the same rocky path you've treaded round and round the last few years. Whenever you see a pattern in your life where the same cycles continually repeat themselves, you

> *The first step to understanding the central truth of the Bread Test— that man "lives by every word that proceeds from the mouth of God"—is to humble ourselves.*

have to humble yourself and ask how it is you keep ending up back at the same old fork in the road.

This is why understanding the bread test is vitally important. This is the first test you will have to pass in order to move into the next season. It doesn't matter how anointed, gifted, called, popular, or wealthy you are—how young, old, good-looking, or qualified you are. It doesn't matter what kind of abuse, torment, or ridicule you've suffered. What matters is whether or not you pass the bread test. Jesus, "God's Anointed," had to pass the bread test. Jesus had to come to the place where He was tempted to rely on His ability to turn stone into bread—or it could have been turning bricks into gold—yet He was able to resist the temptation by living by the Word of God: *"Man does not live by bread alone, but by every word that proceeds from the mouth of God."*

> *The words that God speaks to you before you go into the wilderness are a clue to your ticket out; they are the words that will sustain you and ultimately bring you victory over the enemy.*

Jesus lived by the very words that proceeded out of God's mouth; He did not just quote them haphazardly. The words He lived by in the wilderness were the last words He heard God speak over Him at the Jordan River just before He was led into the wilderness: *"You are My beloved Son."* These were the words that Jesus lived by, and they were the words that satan so vehemently challenged. The words that God speaks to you before you go into the wilderness are a clue to your ticket out; they are the words that will sustain you and ultimately bring you victory over the enemy.

Do not make the same mistake the children of Israel did when they found themselves in the wilderness. They did not discern the words that God spoke over them and so went *"astray in their heart"* (Heb. 3:10). They were inflicted with *"an evil heart of unbelief in departing from the living God"* (Heb. 3:12) and were unable to hear the voice of God. You must be careful to heed the words that God speaks over you and to live by them: *"If you will hear His voice, do not harden your hearts as in the rebellion"* (Heb. 3:15).

Develop the ability to discern God's voice. The words God speaks to you are life—just as His written Word is living and powerful. *You can recognize the words God speaks to you personally by knowing what God spoke in His written Word.* Jesus' reliance on the authority of the written Word released a new level of strength in Him—a strength that went beyond His own physical ability. He showed God that He would live by the standard of His

Word no matter what. This same opportunity is available to you. When you rely on God's Word to overcome temptation, you develop spiritual strength. You develop an authority—an earned authority that positions and propels you toward your destiny in Christ. When you pass the bread test, your authority expands. You can be trusted because of your complete reliance on God. You begin to move toward your seat of authority; you are positioning yourself for blessing because you have aligned every decision you make, every word you speak, every thought you think with every Word that proceeds out of the mouth of God. God begins to hold out His scepter toward you; He can look toward you and decree something to you that no enemy can prevail against because you have situated yourself in your appointed place of authority.

> *When you rely on God's Word to overcome temptation, you develop spiritual strength.*

There is nothing more powerful than spiritual authority. And that authority is wielded in the spirit by words. Life is in the Word. We live by His every Word. The Hebrew for *mouth* used in Deuteronomy 8:3, *"from the mouth of the Lord,"* is not referring to the natural organ we use to chew our food. The root of the Hebrew word used here is in relation to the breath—or wind—of the voice of God. So essentially the Scripture is saying, "We live by the breath of God; we live by every word that is blown out of the mouth of God by His Spirit or through His breath." It is this God-breathed-Spirit-Word that sustains life.

Are you sustained by your job, by the money in your bank account, by your talent or credentials, or are you sustained by the living, breathing Word of God? Now why is that so important? Because even the bread you eat—even the seed in the ground that yields the wheat to make that bread—exists because it proceeded from God's mouth. In Genesis we read that God spoke and the Word that went from His mouth created everything we see and don't see in the heavens and on the earth. We know Jesus is that Word, the ultimate Bread of Life in whom *"we live and move and have our being"* (Acts 17:28). God the Father sent His Son, the Bread from Heaven, to nourish and sustain us. As Jesus said Himself, *"I am the bread of life. He who comes to Me shall never hunger, and he who believes in Me shall never thirst"* (John 6:35). And again later on, Jesus explained it this way:

> *I am the bread of life. Your fathers ate the manna in the wilderness, and are dead. This is the bread which comes down from heaven that one may eat of it and not die.*

*I am the living bread which came down
from heaven. If anyone eats of this bread,
he will live forever; and the bread that I
shall give is My flesh, which I shall give for
the life of the world* (John 6:48-51).

Remember, Jesus taught that if you're not faithful with unrighteous mammon, you can't be trusted with the true riches of the Kingdom. That's the bread test. If you submit to God and worship Him alone, mammon will submit to you. But if you worship mammon, you will end up being its slave for the rest of your life. You will never be free from the enemy because you will never make it to the safety of your seat of authority under the protection of the sovereign hand of God.

Once you pass the bread test, however, you have taken your first step on your way out of the wilderness. Passing the bread test qualifies you to take your seat of authority because God has tried your heart. The greater your authority, the greater the trials you will endure in the wilderness. The greater the temptations you overcome, the more authority you will have earned. Once you make it to your seat, God wants to be sure you have what it takes to stay there.

If you've been in the wilderness for the past several years, it could be that you have been there too long.

Remember the Spirit of God may lead you into the wilderness but you can keep yourself there. When God leads you into the wilderness it is not judgment and the proof is that when you are in the wilderness you have many encounters with His Presence and you experience visitations, supernatural provision and miracles. You will develop a deep intimacy with God in the wilderness and learn to appreciate the pillar of fire by night and cloud by day. In the wilderness you have to live on miracles but when you come out of the wilderness God makes you the miracle unto others. Get a handle on the bread test, get it right in your life, and God will give you authority in that particular area. He will give you something to steward. When you pass the bread test, God will trust you with bread for others as you walk in His Kingdom assignment for you.

> *If you submit to God and worship Him alone, mammon will submit to you. But if you worship mammon, you will end up being its slave for the rest of your life.*

### The Identity Test

> *Then the devil took Him up into the holy city, set Him on the pinnacle of the temple,*

*and said to Him, "If You are the Son of God, throw Yourself down. For it is written: 'He shall give His angels charge over you,' and, 'In their hands they shall bear you up, Lest you dash your foot against a stone.'" Jesus said to him, "It is written again, 'You shall not tempt the Lord your God'"* (Matthew 4:5-7).

As soon as Jesus passed the bread test, satan threw down his next challenge. He dared Him to prove His identity, *"If You are the Son of God, throw Yourself down."* He provoked Him by quoting Scripture, *"For it is written: 'He shall give His angels charge over you.'"* Why wouldn't Jesus prove Himself? Why wouldn't He display His glory? I'll tell you why: because a true Son doesn't have anything to prove. Identity is not just who you are but who you are of and if you know Jesus then you are born of God. If you are confident in your identity, you don't need to show off your special talents to prove your worth.

> *If you are confident in your identity, you don't need to show off your special talents to prove your worth.*

Interestingly, this has been a challenge that the

Church has repeatedly failed in the last 40 years. In the 1967, with the beginning of the Charismatic movement, there was an emphasis on the gifts of the Spirit. It was a type of spiritual awakening—a widespread acknowledgment that the gifts of the Spirit are evidence of God at work in the modern church. This was an exciting move of the Spirit. The gifts of the Spirit are certainly a blessing.

What has happened since that time is that the Church has become distracted with trying to prove the validity of the gift rather than embracing the Gift-Giver. But the focus is going to be shifted back to knowing and worshiping God. We are entering an era when the Church will again pursue the Spirit, as well as the fruit of the Spirit. In First Corinthians 14:1 we are exhorted to, *"Pursue love, and desire spiritual gifts,"* yet for too long we have largely pursued gifts while scarcely desiring love. Although spiritual gifts are still to be deeply desired and will even increase, the focus of our attention should be on the love of God and the God of love.

Part of passing the identity test is passing the gift test. Is your gift going to be the thing that defines you? Is your identity wrapped up in your gift? This is exactly how the devil challenged Jesus in the wilderness. Satan tried to get Jesus to show off His gift—to use it to suit His own purposes. But Jesus understood that He didn't need His gift to sustain Him any more than He needed bread. You can worship the gift in the same way you worship mammon—or bread—or whatever your provision happens to be. The gifts, abilities, and privileges He endows you with can become idols that keep you from the God who bestows them.

I thank God for the gifts He has blessed me with, but the gifts are not for my own personal growth and development. They are for the purpose of blessing other people—helping others grow and develop. As for me, I must build my life on what will strengthen and develop me: God's Word. I choose to trust the *Word* of God that is working *in* me rather than the *gifts* of God that are working *through* me. This is key to passing the identity test. Once you establish your identity in Christ, no devil will have power over you, no person will keep you from taking your seat of authority, and nothing will be able to interfere with your destiny.

> *I choose to trust the **Word** of God that is working in me rather than the gifts of God that are working **through** me. This is key to passing the identity test.*

These are some things that you have to learn in the wilderness. If you're saying, "God, I'm gifted; God, I'm anointed; God, I'm this and I'm that," it doesn't sound like you're humbled enough yet. When you begin to say, "God, *You* are great; God, You're awesome; God, You're amazing," then you are on your way. You can't say to the devil when he comes to you, "I'm gifted!" Jesus wasted no time recalling the word God spoke over Him: *"This is My beloved Son, in whom I am well pleased"* (Matt. 3:17).

### Identity Versus Purpose

When Jesus was anointed and called out by God, there was no complicated prophecy regarding His gifting and purpose. There was no divine assignment given forth. God simply announced, *"This is My beloved Son."* That's all He said. Often we hear a message about the gift God has called us to and we immediately feel we have to go out and stir up the gift. Sooner or later our identity becomes wrapped up in that effort. Satan will convince us to promote our gift out of a hunger to define our purpose. We become so desperate to clarify our purpose that we don't hear the word God speaks over us concerning who we are.

Like many people, you might be in a place in your life crying out to the Father, "God, reveal Your purpose to me; show me what I'm called to do." You've got something in your heart, you are pregnant with purpose, but you don't know how to move forward. How often do you have a revelation about what you should be doing but don't know how to begin applying it? You've got something growing within you that wants to come out, and so you're pushing saying, "Father, show me Your purpose."

Yet all you hear is, "My Son, I love you with an everlasting love. You are made in My image; you were created in Christ Jesus, foreordained unto good works." (See Jeremiah 31:3, Genesis 1:27, and Ephesians 2:10.)

You excitedly reply, "Father, what's the good work?"

And you hear, "I've numbered every hair on your head, when you walk through the valley of the shadow of death, My rod and staff will comfort you. My righteousness will go before you, and My glory will be your rear guard." (See Matthew 10:30, Psalm 23:4, and Isaiah 58:8.)

"Hallelujah! But where am I going? What am I supposed to be doing? What is my purpose?"

Every time you ask the Father for purpose, He'll speak identity to you. "My son, *who you are* is more important than what you're going to do. Because if I reveal My purpose to you before you have a firm grasp on your identity, your purpose will replace—or overshadow—your identity." When your purpose replaces your identity, you have to continually strive toward your purpose. Your identity becomes defined by what you do instead of who God has said that you are. The day you fail to achieve your purpose, you feel as though you cease to exist; you look in the mirror and don't recognize the beloved child of God that

He has called you to be. What you have become is a servant of God when He called you to be a son. A servant is traced by his works, while a child is traced by his DNA. If you want to identify a son or daughter, you check their DNA and see if it matches up with the parent's.

> *Don't forget who you are: "God's beloved." And then remember, that's all you need to know.*

The Bible says that if you are born in Christ, you are born of God. The first thing satan will come to attack in the wilderness is your identity. The first two tests he uses to tempt Jesus begin with, *"If You are the Son of God."* You have to be absolutely certain of who you are in Christ.

The first thing you do when you are tempted by the devil is say, "Lord, I'm going to live by Your Word concerning my identity."

Satan will try to deceive you by causing you to question your purpose. If he can distract you with a desire for your purpose rather than a desire for God, or get you to focus on your gifts, even the gifts of the Spirit, rather than focusing on your identity, he can keep you on that circular journey round and round the same big rocks. Don't forget who you are: "God's beloved." And then remember, that's all you need to know.

We are comparing spiritual things with spiritual things, identity is important and so is purpose and gifting and anointing but we must know and understand the way of God concerning these things.

### The Authority Test

> *Again, the devil took Him up on an exceedingly high mountain, and showed Him all the kingdoms of the world and their glory. And he said to Him, "All these things I will give You if You will fall down and worship me." Then Jesus said to him, "Away with you, Satan! For it is written, 'You shall worship the Lord your God, and Him only you shall serve'"* (Matthew 4:8-10).

After Jesus passes the bread test and then the identity test, the devil makes his biggest challenge of all. He takes Jesus up on an *"exceedingly high mountain, and showed Him all the kingdoms of the world and their glory."* He then makes his final offer, *"All these things I will give You if You will fall down and worship me."* Here Jesus had come to reign in the earth, to reclaim His authority and take back dominion for mankind. Satan gives Him the opportunity to fulfill His destiny *without suffering for it.*

He is offering to give Jesus all that He had come for without the cross.

When this test is placed before Jesus, He is not in His seat of authority. Jesus has not yet gone to the synagogue where He sits down in His seat. All He has is the Word of God. Many of you have had a word from God. You have been called and appointed, and of course you are gifted, so you are preparing to do something great. Here Jesus has nothing but a word. Now remember He's been in the wilderness starving for 40 days. He is tempted to think like you or I would, "Let me see if I can exercise my gift right now and show you what it's all about. Maybe my gift can transport me out of this wilderness; maybe my gift can transfer me out of this prison; maybe my gift can deliver me out of the lions' den; maybe my gift can get me out of this cave."

There's a whole generation of people who are susceptible to being bought, to being owned, to being in a position of compromise when an opportunity is given to fulfill their destiny. But Jesus knew something; He knew He couldn't fulfill His assignment without occupying His seat. The enemy knew that Jesus had the potential to take away his seat, so he attempted to make a deal with Him—to form an alliance. If the enemy cannot get you to fail the bread test or the identity test, he will try to buy you off, usually through another person. He will convince you to take a shortcut by making an unholy alliance. *There is no shortcut to destiny!*

Remember how important it is for you to make it to your seat in order to fulfill your assignment, and how once you get to your seat all that you need is going to come to you. But if you don't get to your seat because you've made an unholy alliance, God can't put you there because the party you have covenanted with will get the power of your seat rather than you. The temptation put before Jesus was intended to compromise His authority.

In Matthew 4:8-10 we watch as Jesus navigates this test of authority and avoids the pitfall of ambition that was evident here too. Notice that the enemy offers Him all the kingdoms of the world. Now ambition is like passion on the surface. But ambition is of the soul and passion is of the spirit. Ambition is about *your* vision, while passion is about *His* vision. Ambition is about climbing over others and doing whatever it takes to exalt yourself, while passion is about laying down your life in the service of others so God can be exalted.

In the corporate world they teach you about ambition. The more ambitious you are, the more they want to pay you. The way of the Kingdom is very different. The Greek word used in the New Testament for *passion* comes from the same word as *suffering*. That's the difference between passion and ambition. *Passion* is "suffering for a purpose—for a prophetic revelation of the heart of God." If you're willing to have that kind of passion, then you will see life come within your spirit and enter the realm of your soul. It will revitalize you. This "resurrection" life is what empowers you to overcome, just like the apostle Paul and Jesus did.

You will be tested for whether your motivation is rooted in ambition or passion. God is so good that He will let you take these tests again and again until you get them right. Until the day of the test, He will tell you everything, trying to give you a hint at all that will be on the test ahead of time. But on the day of the test, His lips are sealed. You might find yourself in the midst of a test crying out, "God, speak to me!" And all you will hear God saying is, "I already spoke to you! Are you going to live by the Word I have spoken?"

Remember the words that God has spoken over you in His Word; remember who you are in Christ, and answer every temptation with authority. Listen to how Jesus responds to satan's offer in Matthew 4:10: *"Away with you, Satan! For it is written, 'You shall worship the Lord your God, and Him only you shall serve.'"* Jesus was clear on what was written, on His identity, and the importance of protecting His authority. He had already set His intention on living by the Word of God, obeying His commands, and worshiping and serving God alone. You need to be equally clear and single-minded about your objectives. That clarity will direct every answer you give and every decision you make; it will make straight your path out of the wilderness.

## POWER AND DISCERNMENT

*Then Jesus returned in the power of the Spirit to Galilee, and news of Him went out through all the surrounding region (Luke 4:14).*

Once you pass the three wilderness tests—the bread test, the identity test, and the authority test—you will be endued with fresh power. That power is a result of fully submitting to God, humbling yourself to the degree that you rely entirely on His Word and on who you are in Him, and being fully satisfied with worshiping and serving God alone. When you can let go of your personal agenda, your ambitions, abilities, and resources, as well as your insecurities, you will walk in the power of the Spirit. You will find yourself promoted out of the wilderness and into the favor of God.

Look what happened to Jesus after He passed the final test in the wilderness. In Luke 4:14-15 we read: "Then Jesus returned in the power of the Spirit to Galilee, and news of Him went out through all the surrounding region. And He taught in their synagogues, being glorified by all." He stepped out into full-time ministry, teaching and preaching all over the region. The power of the Spirit was upon Him, and He was "glorified by all." However, keep in mind that He had not yet sat down in His seat of authority.

This can be a very confusing place. Although you are walking in a degree of power, this power is not for the purpose of fulfilling your assignment. When the power of the Spirit comes, doors will start to open and opportunities will present themselves that you have been waiting a long time for. The common mistake people make at this point is thinking, "It's time! Let's go! Let's do it!" But the reason you are experiencing a degree of power in your life is so that you can make it to your seat of authority.

> *He had already set His intention on living by the Word of God, obeying His commands, and worshiping and serving God alone. You need to be equally clear and single-minded about your objectives.*

It's one thing to know it's a new season, but you have to discern some things when you're on the brink of that new season. You are no longer discerning between good and evil as you did in the wilderness. When you are walking in the power and favor of God and things are lining up around you to propel you forward, it is no longer about what is wrong or right—what is dark and light—but what is good and what is God. Whenever you're on the verge of a new season, many opportunities will open up before you and you will have to choose what is a God thing over what is just a good thing.

> *When you are walking in the power and favor of God and things are lining up around you to propel you forward, it is no longer about what is wrong or right—what is dark and light—but what is good and what is God.*

In Luke 4:14-15, although we see the Spirit of God empowering Jesus, He does not get distracted by this new spiritual power working through Him. Jesus knew that the purpose for this power was to get Him to His seat of authority so that He could fulfill His assignment. He was not trying to build a big ministry or make contacts. There was still one more thing He had to do. He had to go to Nazareth, enter the synagogue, and take His seat.

In Luke 4:16, Jesus arrives in Nazareth *"where He had been brought up"* and goes to the synagogue on the Sabbath as was His custom. It is here that He is handed the

Book of Isaiah from which He reads the famous passage from chapter 61:

> *The Spirit of the Lord is upon Me, because He has anointed Me to preach the gospel to the poor; He has sent Me to heal the brokenhearted, to proclaim liberty to the captives and recovery of sight to the blind, to set at liberty those who are oppressed; to proclaim the acceptable year of the Lord* (Luke 4:18-19).

Then Jesus ceremoniously closes the book, returns it to the attendant, and sits down. "And the eyes of all who were in the synagogue were fixed on Him. And He began to say to them, 'Today this Scripture is fulfilled in your hearing'" (Luke 4:20-21). *It is at this point that Jesus takes His seat of authority.*

He is now positioned under the hand of God to do the work of the Kingdom. He is seated under the protection of God's sovereignty. Nothing on the earth, nor above or below it, can prevail against Him. He is firmly established in His seat. Yet although He is walking in the fullness of God's sovereign authority, there is something else that governs His actions. This is probably the most challenging of all the tests. It was the test that qualified

Jesus to enter the wilderness in the first place. If He had not passed this test, He would not have been baptized and called out by God and subsequently driven into the wilderness by the Holy Spirit. If He had not proven His power in this particular area, He would never have achieved His eternal purpose.

If Jesus did not possess the power to fully submit to every earthly authority regardless of how unjust, there would be no cross.

### *The Submission Test*

> *Jesus came from Galilee to John at the Jordan to be baptized by him. And John tried to prevent Him, saying, "I need to be baptized by You, and are You coming to me?" But Jesus answered and said to him, "Permit it to be so now, for thus it is fitting for us to fulfill all righteousness"* (Matthew 3:13-15).

Earlier we mentioned that when Jesus was baptized the heavens opened and God declared that this was His beloved Son in whom He was well pleased. What compelled God at this point to make such an announcement?

Let's look at what happened just prior to Jesus being

baptized. In Matthew 3:13-15 we read that Jesus came looking for John the Baptist. When John sees Jesus, he immediately recognizes Him declaring, *"Behold! The Lamb of God who takes away the sin of the world!"* (John 1:29). John tells Jesus, "I'm not worthy to baptize You. You should be baptizing me!" Yet Jesus submits to John's authority by asking him to *"permit it to be so now, for thus it is fitting for us to fulfill all righteousness."*

John the Baptist did not fully understand what Jesus was doing here, but Jesus knew, and He understood the importance of acknowledging the authority of others. Even though He *"who, being in the form of God...made Himself of no reputation...humbled Himself and became obedient to the point of death, even the death of the cross"* (Phil. 2:6-8) could have ignored protocol, He sought it out instead. He begins this journey of holy submission—which would ultimately lead to His crucifixion—by submitting to the authority of John the Baptist. It is after this initial test that His Father announced from Heaven, "Yes! This My beloved Son in whom I am well pleased!"

What launched Jesus onto the road of authority was

> *What launched Jesus onto the road of authority was having mastered the art of submission.*

having mastered the art of submission. He demonstrated that He understood how to respect the authority of others and the significance that held if He hoped to walk in any authority of His own. There are some of you who may be in some troublesome places regarding authority. Your father may have abused you, you may have suffered injustice by those in authority over you at work or in your church, and even though you have forgiven the individuals, you still have a tainted perspective of authority. Every time you hear the word *authority*, or the word *submit*, you cringe because your perception of submission is that it is going to violate and take advantage of you.

God, on the other hand, views the concept of submission as a means of blessing. In Proverbs 10:6 (KJV) we read that *"blessings are upon the head of the just."* Whenever you see the word *head* in the Bible, it is referring to an authority through which blessing flows. *Authority* in this context is an avenue for blessing. Think of Second Timothy 2:21 (TM), which talks about being a vessel of honor—or authority—set aside for the sole purpose of good works: *"the kind of container God can use to present any and every kind of gift to His guests for their blessing."* Think of the dew of Hermon from Psalm 133 we talked about earlier that flows from the top of the head—from the place of authority—down over the body. This is how God's authority works. It is a channel of blessing.

Keep this in mind as we look at Romans 13:1 ESV: "Let every person be subject to the governing authorities. For there is no authority except from God, and those that exist have been instituted by God." This is actually the main reason why some powerfully gifted and anointed people are never able to make it to their seat and therefore fulfill their assignment. Read what we are told in the very next verse: "Therefore whoever resists the authority resists the ordinance of God, and those who resist will bring judgment on themselves" (Rom. 13:2).

Keep that in mind as you read First Peter 2:18-20:

> *Servants, be submissive to your masters with all fear, not only to the good and gentle, but also to the harsh. For this is commendable, if because of conscience toward God one endures grief, suffering wrongfully. For what credit is it if, when you are beaten for your faults, you take it patiently? But when you do good and suffer, if you take it patiently, this is commendable before God.*

In John 19, Jesus is taken before Pilate after He has been scourged and beaten. We read in verse 10 where

Pilate says to Him, *"Do You not know that I have power to crucify You, and power to release You?"*

Jesus answers, "You could have no power at all against Me unless it had been given you from above" (John 19:11). Jesus, at the threshold of His execution, respects Pilate's seat of authority. In verse 13, we read that Pilate "brought Jesus out and sat down in the judgment seat." Pilate had to sit in his seat of authority to declare his judgment concerning Jesus.

When you are in your seat of authority, you have the power to pass judgment, make decrees, and influence the region that God has put you in jurisdiction over. Jesus submits to the judgment Pilate decrees from his seat of authority. He recognizes Pilate's position as governor of the province and submits to it. Jesus, the Lord of lords and King of kings, submits to an unjust earthly authority to the point of death. You can be assured that if He was required to submit in this way, then so are you. You must understand that regardless of whether you have a certain seat of authority, you must esteem the seats of others.

Do you remember in First Corinthians 11:29-30 where it talks about many being sick and weak because they have not properly discerned the Body of Christ? Yes, we must recognize that the Lord's body was broken so we could be whole, but we must also discern the Body of

Christ in regards to the Church in the earth today. The Church is the Body of Christ. Within this Body, God has positioned people in places of authority, and we must discern and respect those seats of authority. Even if someone in authority has sinned, it is not our job to ridicule and correct this person. It is God's job.

Think about what David went through at the hands of Saul. David was running for his life, hiding out in a cave, doing everything possible to placate his soldiers who were ready to overthrow Saul and place David on the throne. At one point, David and his soldiers find themselves in the back of the same cave as Saul. David, prompted by his men, takes his sword and cuts off a portion of Saul's garment while he's otherwise occupied. David could have killed Saul, yet he finds himself ashamed for doing even this small thing.

In this instance, Saul is God's tool to prepare David for his seat of authority. God keeps Saul in his seat long enough to make sure David passes this test of the heart. David's ability to submit in this case will lay the foundation for every other decision he makes. You see, God is about to give David a seat that is so significant that He had to be sure he could harness the power of submission. The seat God had prepared for David was the same throne of authority Jesus is destined to sit on when He returns to reign on the earth. (See First Samuel 24:1-6.)

This seat is so important that David had to be given the same test twice! In First Samuel 26:7-9 we read about another opportunity David had to remove Saul. Saul is asleep with his men because of a deep sleep that fell on them from the Lord. To the undiscerning heart it seemed like God had made a way for David to take out his enemy.

*You don't have to be afraid of the wilderness, but you can be prepared.*

So when David's servant says, "God has delivered your enemy into your hand this day. Now therefore, please, let me strike him at once with the spear, right to the earth; and I will not have to strike him a second time," David replies, "Do not destroy him; for who can stretch out his hand against the Lord's anointed, and be guiltless?" In other words, he says, "I will live by the word, the revelation, the conviction that the Spirit gave me; I will not touch God's anointed." Not too long after this, Saul died by falling on his own sword in battle.

Passing each of these wilderness tests is part of the process of aligning yourself with God's plumb line. There are seasons you must go through that will prepare and position you to walk in the place of authority God has destined for you. You don't have to be afraid of the wilderness, but you can be prepared. I encourage you to boldly face each test with confidence. You have the Spirit of God, the mind of Christ, the name of Jesus, and the Word of the Father working on your behalf. Step out in faith knowing that each test is a milestone on your path to promise.

> *My brethren, count it all joy when you fall into various trials, knowing that the testing of your faith produces patience. But let patience have its perfect work, that you may be perfect and complete, lacking nothing* (James 1:2-4).

## ☙ GETTING IN POSITION ❧

The path to promise always leads through the wilderness. Jesus, God's own beloved Son, was led straight into the wilderness after He was baptized.

- Why did the Spirit of God drive Jesus into the wilderness?
- If God led Jesus into the wilderness, why might God lead you there too?

The first thing satan tempted Jesus to do after 40 days in the desert was to turn stones into bread.

- Why is it significant that satan tempted Jesus to turn bread into stones before tempting Him to do anything else?
- What does it mean to live "by every word that proceeds out of the mouth of God?"

Satan then dared Jesus to prove His identity.

- Why didn't Jesus display His glory?
- Is your identity wrapped up in your gifts or abilities?
- How can you make sure you will pass the "identity test?"

If the enemy cannot get you to fail the bread test or the identity test, he will try to convince you to take a shortcut to fulfilling your assignment.

- Where have you been tempted to take shortcuts in moving closer to your destiny?

# CHAPTER 6

# PREPARING FOR BATTLE

*So it came about, on the day of battle, that there was neither sword nor spear found in the hand of any of the people who were with Saul and Jonathan. But they were found with Saul and Jonathan his son*
(1 Samuel 13:22).

We are on the verge of a great day of battle. The front lines of the Kingdom of God are beginning to advance like never before. The hand of the Lord will come upon His people and rapidly accelerate their gifts and callings; every branch and manifestation of the Kingdom will be released with renewed power. God's people are going to be positioned and re-positioned in places of authority within the Church as well as in every area of society. We will see the government of God begin to take shape. We're moving into an age of faith and authority such that when the name of Jesus is spoken, nothing will remain the same. When God's Word is spoken, it will bring transformation to every area of life, tear down every stronghold, and empower every believer even more than it has in the past.

God is establishing a new dimension of Kingdom authority in the earth—a new Kingdom order that will require some switching of roles and changes in leadership. You will see a change of guard taking place throughout the Church. You will also begin to see how God is equipping and training His people for combat. He is preparing His people so they will not be ignorant of the enemy's strategies—so they will be skilled in the art of spiritual warfare and prepared for every battle ahead.

The training ground for God's Army will initially take place in the Church. In fact, there will be some skirmishes within the Church as well. The first confrontations will be among the various church leaders as God makes some Kingdom-scale adjustments. As in the time of Saul and David, the battle for authority will begin in the palace. There was a period of time when King Saul, his heir Jonathan, and the gifted David dwelled together in peace. Each held the promise of leadership. Yet, as each grew in their calling, there was a testing that took place, and friction developed between Saul and David. Ultimately the house was divided. Throughout this process, God was repositioning His Kingdom's leadership. We can look back and see which type of leadership prevailed and why, and learn some things about what God is doing in His Kingdom today.

> *We can look back and see which type of leadership prevailed and why, and learn some things about what God is doing in His Kingdom today.*

I believe there are three categories of leadership in the Church, which have divided God's people into three different camps. It is between these three camps that God is about to make some shifts. There will be a repositioning much like we saw happen during the reign of King Saul just before David took the throne. Note that this is only the beginning. When this repositioning took place—this battle for leadership—King David's reign had yet to begin. You could say that this difficult period of realignment represents that darkest hour just before the dawn. It's as if all of Israel waited with David in the dark depths of a cave before emerging to take authority in the earth.

## THE SAULISTIC ORDER

*And Saul said to Samuel… "But the people took of the plunder, sheep and oxen, the best of the things which should have been utterly destroyed, to sacrifice to the Lord your God in Gilgal"* (1 Samuel 15:20-21).

There is a model of leadership from this era that God is dealing with right now. This type of leadership is what I call the "Saulistic model of leadership." To understand this leadership style, we have but to look at Saul's heart. In First Samuel 10:9 we read that the Lord gives Saul a new heart, yet once Saul steps into his place of authority, his heart becomes increasingly hardened. By reading further, we see what lies at the foundation of Saul's problem; it is what remains imbedded in his heart: a fear of what people think.

> *We see what lies at the foundation of Saul's problem; it is what remains imbedded in his heart: a fear of what people think.*

Throughout the remaining chapters of First Samuel we repeatedly come across the phrase *"but the people."* Saul was afraid of what others thought. Because he sought to please people rather than God, his authority was perverted; his capacity to judge and make wise decisions became distorted. His God-given leadership ability grew gradually more defective because he increasingly feared other's opinions more than God's.

In First Samuel 15:20-21 we see Saul's heart revealed in three distinct ways. He not only allows *"the people"* to do what they think is best by taking *"the plunder, sheep and oxen, the best of the things... to sacrifice to the Lord your God in Gilgal"*—but he is quick to point the finger of blame. He does not take responsibility for the actions of his people. Not only that, notice that when he is speaking to Samuel he uses the words, *"your God."* Saul does not have a revelation of God being *his* sovereign Lord; he is more concerned about justifying himself before Samuel than proving his faith and trust in God. To this Samuel replies:

> *Has the Lord as great delight in burnt offerings and sacrifices, as in obeying the voice of the Lord? Behold, to obey is better than sacrifice, and to heed than the fat of rams. For rebellion is as the sin of witchcraft, and stubbornness is as iniquity and idolatry. Because you have rejected the word of the Lord, He also has rejected you from being king* (1 Samuel 15:22-23).

Saul becomes complacent, and then disobedient, and finally rebellious. He rejects the word of the Lord and so the Lord rejects him. Saul is an example of a man chosen by God who miserably fails the bread test. He lives by everything *but* the Word of the Lord. He idolizes power, popularity, and prestige—all based in his desire to please people, to be loved by people rather than God. Saul never actually makes it out of the wilderness of his own vanity and pride. He is deceived by a passionless ambition, an identity-corroding purpose, and a prideful conceit. He loses sight of who it is God has called him to be because he is more enamored with the gifts God has given him than with obeying His directives.

As a result of this underlying fear of man, Saul becomes even more insecure, and that insecurity brings about a self-deceiving pride that eats like a cancer at his soul. This pride fed a consuming jealousy that gave way to a murderous spirit. Saul was jealous of David's giftedness and anointing; he felt threatened and intimidated by his very presence. He may have even been jealous of his own son Jonathan for the same reasons. After Jonathan secures a tremendous victory for Israel early in the war against the Philistines, Saul threatens to have him killed for violating a command he didn't even know about. In First Samuel 14:24-46 we read where Jonathan put a little honey to his lips after Saul commanded that no one should eat and for this Saul determines he should be executed.

There is an entire generation of Saul-like leaders in the Church who either feel threatened by the abilities of those around them, or are simply ignorant of their potential. There is a pervasive inability to perceive and value the call of God on the next generation of leaders God is raising up. A Saulistic generation refuses to acknowledge the great potential in people like David who have come of age, or a whole generation of people like Jonathan who are waiting in the wings. Saul-like leaders are more interested in building their own kingdoms than the Kingdom of God.

Interestingly, in a Saulistic order, as we read in First Samuel 13:22, no one has a sword except Saul and his own sons. Under Saul's leadership, the Philistines kidnap the blacksmiths that make the weaponry so that Saul's kingdom is left with no sword or spear—two very important weapons in the time of battle. Only the house of Saul is allowed to keep their swords. What begins to happen is that as the battle lines are drawn, the people are not in a position to fight, so they have to rely on Saul to fight their battles for them. (See First Samuel 13:16-22.)

Sadly, Saul relies more on the power of his sword than he does on the power of His Lord. He puts his trust in his gifts and position. Because Saul puts his trust in his own sword, he dies by his own sword—as Jesus said, *"All who draw the sword will die by the sword"* (Matt. 26:52).

## WHERE'S THE BEEF?

*For though by this time you ought to be teachers, you need someone to teach you again the first principles of the oracles of God; and you have come to need milk and not solid food. For everyone who partakes only of milk is unskilled in the word of righteousness, for he is a babe. But solid food belongs to those who are of full age, that is, those who by reason of use have their senses exercised to discern both good and evil* (Hebrews 5:12-15).

When you first come into the Kingdom of God, when you are a young babe in Christ, you need to be fed with the milk of the Word as Peter teaches in First Peter 2:2, *"As newborn babes, desire the pure milk of the word, that you may grow thereby."* The milk of the Word you receive as a new believer provides the building blocks upon which you develop your faith and grow—the key word here being *grow*. In order to do that, you must develop your capacity to digest more than just milk. Hebrews 6:1-2 explains it this way:

> *Therefore, leaving the discussion of the elementary principles of Christ, let us go on to perfection, not laying again the foundation of repentance from dead works and of faith toward God, of the doctrine of baptisms, of laying on of hands, of resurrection of the dead, and of eternal judgment.*

These are the first principles in growing in the knowledge of Christ; but now God is saying it's time to be weaned from the milk and move on to the meat of the Word in order to grow and develop.

The goal is that you become skilled in the word of righteousness. What is the word of righteousness? We are told in Ephesians 6:17 that it is the sword of the Spirit, which is the Word of God. Most of us, as we just read, never become skilled in the word of righteousness because we only partake of the milk. We are never able to skillfully wield the sword of the Spirit because we haven't grown strong enough for lack of solid food. This is what happens under a Saulistic type of leadership. The people remain unskilled with the sword of the Spirit—or the Word of God—so that in the time of battle they are unprepared to fight.

Like the people under Saul, there are people in the Church today who are in crisis and they don't know what to do. They don't know how to deal with adversity or any kind of opposition because they don't understand how to wield the Word of God; they don't fully grasp that *"the word of God is living and powerful, and sharper than any two-edged sword"* (Heb. 4:12)!

As God is positioning you in your place of authority, you will need to learn how to use His Word. In order for you to become skilled with the word of righteousness, you will have to understand it more thoroughly and deeply. You need to move on from just the milk of the Word to the meat of it also. I believe the Spirit of the Lord is looking and asking the Church, "Where's the beef?" Or "Where's the meat?" In order to grow into the army God is calling the Body of Christ to become, we will have to develop the capacity to digest the meat of the Word. Otherwise, we will remain weak, malnourished, immature babes in the spirit.

The enemy is particularly interested in keeping the Church underdeveloped. If he can arrest her growth, she will never be able to speak for herself. Babies are not able to speak. Spiritual infants have no voice in the Kingdom because they are unskilled in the word of righteousness. *"For everyone who partakes only of milk is unskilled in the word of righteousness, for he is a babe"* (Heb. 5:13).

They have no say in what is happening; they are spiritually mute. This is why we must insist on solid food so we can grow and speak out and skillfully wield the sword of the Spirit.

Now under the Saulistic type of leadership, leaders feed the people milk to keep them quiet—to keep them weak but satisfied. This is a picture of what is happening in many churches today. Congregations are satisfied with milk because it is cheap and easy to provide. When it was time for his people to be weaned, Saul created a milk bottle, formulated his own milk, and fed that formula to them to keep them quiet. When they were supposed to be transitioning from milk to solid food, they got stuck on the bottle. In the time of battle, instead of pulling out a sword, they pull out a milk bottle!

Different Saulistic orders create different types of milk. The bottles come in different shapes and sizes, different programs and organizations, but at the end of the day, it is still just milk.

On the other hand, when these babes hear someone who has been fed on meat skillfully speak forth the word of righteousness, they will try to imitate them. They will take what they have heard and attempt to come against the enemy. Look what happened to the seven sons of Sceva in Acts 19:13-16. They witnessed Paul casting out demons in the name of Jesus, so when they came across someone possessed by an evil spirit, they followed suit and said, *"We exorcise you by the Jesus whom Paul preaches."* The evil spirit answered them, *"Jesus I know, and Paul I know; but who are you? Then the man in whom the evil spirit dwelled leaped upon them, overpowered them, and prevailed against them, so that they fled out of that house naked and wounded."* They got beat up because they were unskilled in the word of righteousness. They didn't have revelation; they just had information. Information in the midst of a spiritual crisis doesn't help you; it's a revelation that becomes part of who you are that enables you to stand in the time of battle. God wants you to learn to eat a good steak now and then. He is going to come to your house and ask, "Where's the beef?"

> *When we become people who are nourished with the rich meat of the Word, we will have the vitality and strength we need to develop and mature into the spiritual leaders God has called us all to be.*

God wants His people to be trained and skilled in the word of righteousness.

Let's look at Ephesians 6:10-11 to get a picture of what the meat of the Word will do for the believer. It will cause you to *"be strong in the Lord and in the power of His might."* It will enable you to *"put on the whole armor of God, that you may be able to stand against the wiles of the devil."* It will empower you, *"having done all, to stand."* Paul is talking to meat-eating Christians who are preparing for battle. He is telling them how to fight—how to hold their positions, engage the enemy, and use their swords skillfully without giving ground:

> *Stand therefore, having girded your waist with truth, having put on the breastplate of righteousness, and having shod your feet with the preparation of the gospel of peace; above all, taking the shield of faith with which you will be able to quench all the fiery darts of the wicked one. And take the helmet of salvation, and the sword of the Spirit, which is the word of God; praying always with all prayer and supplication in the Spirit, being watchful to this end with all perseverance and supplication for all the saints* (Ephesians 6:12-18).

Ultimately, we are being told that until we are able to wield the sword of the Spirit with confidence, we cannot even effectively pray. When we become people who are nourished with the rich meat of the Word, we will have the vitality and strength we need to develop and mature into the spiritual leaders God has called us all to be. Then we will be in a position to use the sword of God's Word and see its effect on the world around us.

This is the season we're entering into. We must be prepared and equipped, for the battle is at hand. We will need something more than our milk bottles to survive. Each one of us must become proficient in the word of righteousness—proficiency that comes from a diet in which we develop the capacity to eat the meat that God is putting out. Once we learn to digest and apply the meat of God's Word, we will be able to discern good from evil and align ourselves only with those who truly fear God.

## THE JONATHAN GENERATION

*The battle became fierce against Saul. The archers hit him, and he was severely wounded by the archers. Then Saul said to his armorbearer, "Draw your sword, and thrust me through with it, lest these uncircumcised men come and thrust me through and abuse me." But his armorbearer would not, for he was greatly afraid. Therefore Saul took a sword and fell on it. And when his armorbearer saw that Saul was dead, he also fell on his sword, and died with him. So Saul, his three sons, his armor-bearer, and all his men died together that same day* (1 Samuel 31:3-6).

Sadly, Saul and his sons, along with all of his men, are chased down by the Philistines and killed. We read here that Saul actually kills himself by falling on his own sword. What I want you to see here, however, is not the tragedy of Saul's demise, but of Jonathan's. God has been speaking to me about a Jonathan generation alive in the earth today that is at risk of following a false leader—a Saulistic type of leader—to their death. There is a Jonathan generation now being raised up that is more pregnant with purpose and potential than any other generation that has lived on this earth.

What is the Jonathan generation? The Jonathan generation has been birthed of Saul, but must be fathered by David. They feel a loyalty and an obligation to follow Saul as their father, but doing so will only lead to destruction. At the same time Jonathan's heart is knit with David's—a heart after God's own heart—it is drawn to David, and covenanted with David (see 1 Sam. 13:14; 2 Sam. 1:26). David's heart represents the new kingdom order that Jonathan feels so strongly connected to. Yet although Saul is not making the shift into the new kingdom order,

Jonathan still feels compelled to follow Saul. Here we have a divine tension between the heart that wants to go with David and the head that feels obligated to follow Saul.

David is called of God to lead, he is anointed and gifted, but he is also hiding out in a cave because Saul wants to kill him. There is a generation of Davids and Josephs and Daniels and Ishmaels that need to come out of the cave—the prison, the lion's den, and the wilderness—in order to position themselves in their seats of authority. Why? For the sake of a generation of Jonathans. There is a generation of Jonathans willing to do whatever God would have them do, but there is an absence of Davidic leadership with the kind of Kingdom heart Jonathan longs to connect with.

> *The Jonathan generation is a generation that is pregnant with the purposes of God. They are looking for leaders to show them how to give birth to their own potential.*

The Jonathan generation has been crying out to the Lord, and now the Lord is saying to them, "I am raising up the Davids. I am bringing them out of the caves. I am placing them in their seats of authority so they can empower and father you." The Jonathan generation is a generation that is pregnant with the purposes of God.

They are looking for leaders to show them how to give birth to their own potential. The Saulistic generation, on the other hand, wants to kill the new thing God is doing in order to maintain control. That is why there is a change about to take place in leadership.

However, God wants to first give an opportunity to the Saulistic order to repent. If they will repent, God will promote them and equip them in this next era. However, if they don't, they will be removed. Saul will fall on his own sword and die, a sword which represents the letter of the law that the Saulistic order clings to.

The Saulistic order is all about the *letter* of the law rather than the *spirit* of the law—or the law of love. God is dealing with this order of leadership because it is not about empowering and releasing others. Look at Second Corinthians 3:6 where it says, *"He has made us competent as ministers of a new covenant—not of the letter but of the Spirit; for the letter kills, but the Spirit gives life"* (NIV). When Moses brought the law down from the mount, the children of Israel were worshiping the golden calf. As a result of the law coming down the mountain that day, 3,000 people died—because the letter judges and kills. Notice in Acts 2:41 we read about the day the Spirit came down and 3,000 people were born-again—that is because the Spirit gives life.

Under, Saul, however, the law became so oppressive that during a time of battle, Saul decreed that no one should eat a thing until every enemy soldier was dead. Jonathan happened to be at the front defeating the enemy on behalf of Saul and did not hear the command. After having sent the enemy fleeing, Jonathan came across some honey and put a little to his lips. When Saul found out, Saul determined to kill Jonathan for breaking the law. That's an example of the letter of the law in operation— it would kill its own son to satisfy its sense of justice.

God is seeking to promote those with a Davidic heart of leadership for the sake of a new generation of Jonathans.

The Jonathan generation is in a difficult spot right now; they feel they must follow Saul, but they need to be led by David. If Jonathan follows Saul, Jonathan will die with Saul. If Jonathan follows David, he will live with David. There is a whole generation pregnant with the purposes of God at stake. God, out of His mercy, will deal with this Saulistic order, but He is shifting a new Davidic order into Saul's former place of authority for the express purpose of leading and empowering this generation of Jonathans.

There is a spirit of Saul that is trying to kill the Jonathan generation for the sake of maintaining its own pride. It is blinded by jealousy and competition and refuses to allow the Jonathan generation to rise up. Meanwhile, because Jonathan's heart is pure, he feels duty bound to Saul. Saul is also pressuring and intimidating Jonathan to follow him because he sees the rise of the Davidic order at hand. It is imperative that the Davidic order emerges from the depths of the cave to take its seat of authority—otherwise, the purposes of a generation of Jonathans will be lost.

The Saulistic generation is a false father generation. Sauls are birthed of instructors; Jonathans and Davids are birthed of fathers. Jonathan needs a father. He's had an instructor but hasn't had a father. He needs David to birth him into his spiritual destiny just as Saul birthed him into the kingdom. Look at First Corinthians 4:15, *"You might have ten thousand instructors in Christ, yet you do not have many fathers."* God is raising up fathers; He is calling spiritual fathers to come forth so that they can raise up sons and daughters. This is why there is a shift taking place in leadership. God wants to release people who have the heart of David—who have been in the cave; who have been in the wilderness—and give them places of authority, places that will liberate and give freedom to the Jonathans alive on the earth today.

## THE DAVIDIC KINGDOM ORDER

*David therefore departed from there and escaped to the cave of Adullam. So when his brothers and all his father's house heard it, they went down there to him.*

*And everyone who was in distress, every-one who was in debt, and everyone who was discontented gathered to him. So he became captain over them. And there were about four hundred men with him* (1 Samuel 22:1-2).

David was a natural-born leader. People gravitated toward him. In the above passage we read that the distressed, the indebted, and the discontented *"gathered to him"* after he had escaped to the cave of Adullam. He trained these stragglers up to be mighty men of valor. He knew how to prepare his people for war and to cultivate their potential. This was the anointing upon David—to take a generation that appears to have no hope and empower them with the Spirit of God. He taught and mentored them and raised them up out of the gutters. We read in First Chronicles 12:1-2 that David's men could fight and use a sword with the right hand *and* with the left. They could throw a spear or shoot an arrow one way or the other—*"using both the right hand and the left in hurling stones and shooting arrows with the bow."* God is seeking to raise up a Davidic generation that will train up mighty men and women of war who will be skillful in the word of righteousness and know how to use it like a sword in battle.

The nature and characteristic of a spiritual father is not patterned after natural fathers. A natural father at best can raise up his son to die—that's the best thing a natural father can do. But you see spiritual fathers are not patterned after natural fathers; they are patterned after our heavenly Father. Joseph, who is symbolic of a natural father, raised up Jesus to die; but God, His heavenly Father, raised up Jesus to live. The human nature at best prepares a nice tomb for those they love. When Joseph of Arimathea saw Jesus on the cross, the best he could do was offer Him his tomb. That's all that man knows to do with death.

When your heavenly Father sees you dying, He looks for the tomb you're buried in only so that He can raise you up out of it. That's the nature of a spiritual father: to resurrect you from the ashes and to bring you out from the place of death. This is what the Father is looking to do in our lives. While the Saulistic spirit is all about death, the Davidic Kingdom spirit is about bringing life to what was once thought dead. This is the heart of the Father.

What the Father is doing now is raising up a generation that doesn't need to be instructed again with the elementary principles of His Word. He is raising up a generation that needs to be fathered and mentored in how to discern between good and evil—a generation that hungers for meat and seeks to become skillful in the word of righteousness. The Father's heart has heard the cry come forth from this generation of Jonathans and is about to empower them to do things the world has never seen before—*"and greater works than these he will do"* (John 14:12).

In order for the Jonathan generation to be empowered, however, God must raise up a Davidic order that is willing to be their spiritual fathers. God is challenging the Davids in the Church today to father His Jonathans. According to protocol, it looks like Saul should father them, but just because they give birth to a son does not mean they are suitable fathers. The worst crisis in the earth today is fatherlessness. Because of fatherlessness a whole generation is dying on the battlefield. What the Church is attempting to do in response is offer instruction rather than fathering. A spiritual father does not take the place of the heavenly Father but raises up sons and daughters who are able to take their place as heirs in the Kingdom.

Another characteristic of a spiritual father is that they circumcise their sons. The thing about circumcision is that if you don't cut deep enough, the son can be prone to infection; but if you cut too deep the son can never reproduce at all. The Saulistic generation has cut too deep so that the Jonathans cannot reproduce seed any longer. Sauls build their own kingdoms, and when they die they have no sons to receive their estate. Spiritual fathers, on the other hand, who have a Davidic heart, will circumcise their sons to protect them from infection but not keep them from reproducing.

God circumcises the hearts of those He loves. In Deuteronomy 30:6 we are told that, "The Lord your God will circumcise your heart and the heart of your descendants, to love the Lord your God with all your heart and with all your soul, that you may live." Why does He circumcise our hearts? So that we may live. How does He circumcise our hearts? With the Word because "the word of God is living and powerful, and sharper than any two-edged sword, piercing even to the division of soul and spirit, and of joints and marrow, and is a discerner of the thoughts and intents of the heart" (Heb. 4:12). God is circumcising the soul; He is circumcising your heart so life can come out of you.

> *A spiritual father does not take the place of the heavenly Father but raises up sons and daughters who are able to take their place as heirs in the Kingdom.*

Why do you think God chose circumcision as a token of righteousness in the Old Testament? God had to circumcise man because this is where the seed comes from; it is where the promise is going to be fulfilled. We have a Jonathan generation that is carrying the seed of God's Word but must be circumcised so they can bring it forth. This seed will reproduce generation after generation that will walk in the things of God. Sadly, the instructors in the

Church have not understood how to circumcise. As a result, many have heard the word of promise but are not able to give birth to it in their life.

Today we have a Jonathan generation that has become supernaturally impregnated by the Spirit of God. These Jonathans are in need of spiritual fathers who understand the art of circumcision. Without spiritual fathers to do the intimate work of cutting and cleaning, coaching and caring, the seed within them will die. What does a spiritual father look like? How does a spiritual father cultivate the seed of potential lying dormant in the hearts of a fatherless generation? What kind of man is the Lord looking for to step into this position of authority and accept the responsibility of adoption?

## THE HEART OF DAVID

*The Lord has sought for Himself a man after His own heart, and the Lord has commanded him to be commander over His people* (1 Samuel 13:14).

The Scripture says that man judges a person by looking at their outward appearance, while God looks at their heart. *"For the Lord does not see as man sees; for man looks at the outward appearance, but the Lord looks at the* heart" (1 Sam. 16:7). It is interesting that these were the words spoken by Samuel the prophet when he was looking over Jesse's sons to determine who would be the future king of Israel. As it turns out, David is the only person in the Bible who God said was a *"man after His own heart."* He is the only one God makes this statement about—in spite of David's sin and adultery. Again we read in Acts 13:22:*"I have found David, the son of Jesse, a man after My own heart, who will do all My will."*

> *The secret to coming out of your cave is to have a heart willing do* **all** *for the Lord.*

The secret to coming out of your cave is to have a heart willing do *all* for the Lord. David demonstrated this willingness when he poured out the most precious thing he had been given to honor God. In First Chronicles 11:15-19, we read how David had longed for a drink of water from the well of Bethlehem, which was located in territory occupied by the Philistines. Three of his mightiest risked their lives to sneak through the enemy camp to draw water from the well of Bethlehem for their leader. They rushed back with the water and presented it to David.

David could not bring himself to drink the water because his men had risked their lives to obtain it and because only the One True King was worthy of such honor. David poured out the water as an offering onto the Lord—for his deeper thirst and longing was for the presence of God.

> *O God, You are my God; early will I seek You; my soul thirsts for You; my flesh longs for You in a dry and thirsty land where there is no water. So I have looked for You in the sanctuary, to see Your power and Your glory* (Psalm 63:1-2).

These mighty men were the same men who were once indebted and distressed. David reproduced his own heart in them—a heart that would do all for his King. As a leader, he valued their sacrifice and loyalty, and in the process demonstrated his own humility by honoring the One who really matters. In the eyes of David, God alone was worthy of such honor and loyalty.

David's men were loyal to him because he took responsibility for them. For example, when David sinned against God by numbering his soldiers in order to calculate his own might, he immediately took responsibility for his mistake and stood in the gap on their behalf. God allowed David to choose which judgment would be released: three years of famine, or three months of defeat, or three days of devastation at the hand of the

Lord. David chose three days of divine destruction. When he saw the angel of the Lord poised over Jerusalem with a sword in his hand, he cried out to God and interceded on behalf of the people: *"Was it not I who commanded the people to be numbered? I am the one who has sinned and done evil indeed; but these sheep, what have they done? Let Your hand, I pray, O Lord my God, be against me and against my father's house, but not against Your people that they should be plagued"* (1 Chron. 21:17).

David goes to the threshing floor of Ornan the Jebusite to build an altar and make an offering to God. David offers to buy the entire property for full price, but Ornan, out of honor for the king, offers to give every bit of it to David for free—oxen, wood, wheat, and all. David made this famous reply in First Chronicles 21:23-25: *"I will not take for the Lord what is yours, nor offer burnt offerings that cost me nothing"* (ESV). In other words, *"I'm not going to offer God sacrifices that are no sacrifice"* (TM).

David truly feared the Lord. He was completely transparent before God. David's relationship with God was authentic and sincere; it was not a superficial alliance based on a set of rules. David's whole heart belonged to God and God alone. This sacrificial heart remained with David even after he became king. Yes, David made mistakes, he even willfully sinned, but his heart remained soft and pliable.

Listen to David's heart cry after he sins with Bathsheba. In Psalm 51:1-12, we can feel the ache of his repentant heart. David's personal prayer of repentance was a prophetic prayer on humanity's behalf that God answered for us all. His prayer becomes a blueprint of the grace God extends to all who seek refuge in Christ.

> *Create in me a clean heart, O God, and renew a steadfast spirit within me. Do not cast me away from Your presence, and do not take Your Holy Spirit from me* (Psalm 51:10-11).

As God keeps His covenant with David—and with all David's descendants who are found in Christ—so David keeps his covenant with the descendants of Saul. After David becomes king, he seeks out Jonathan's heir to bless him. This was very unusual because it was not uncommon for a new king to annihilate all trace of the former king's family. When David finds Mephibosheth, the son of Jonathan and the grandson of Saul, he says to him, *"Do not fear, for I will*

> *David's personal prayer of repentance was a prophetic prayer on humanity's behalf that God answered for us all.*

*surely show you kindness for Jonathan your father's sake, and will restore to you all the land of Saul your grandfather; and you shall eat bread at my table continually"* (2 Sam. 9:7). This is a representation of God's heart toward us and the heart we should have toward Jonathan and his heirs.

God is calling His Davids to rise up and seek out the Jonathans to bless them *"for their father's sake"*—to actively pursue them to show them kindness and restore them—to bring them to their supper table and adopt them as sons and heirs. A Davidic kingdom order will establish the sons of Saul as mighty warriors, skilled in the word of righteousness, able to discern between good and evil. As Davids come into their place of authority, they will preserve the Jonathan generation and allow them to receive their inheritance. They will know who they are in Christ; they will have confidence and the boldness required of sons and daughters of God. They will be secure in who they are, their position in the Kingdom, and the hope of their potential.

As David passed the authority test so that he could rise to be king, so will Jonathan be required to pass the identity test so that he can one day inherit the throne.

> *"And you shall not only show me the kindness of the Lord while I still live, that I may not die; but you shall not cut off your*

*kindness from my house forever, no, not when the Lord has cut off every one of the enemies of David from the face of the earth."* (1 Samuel 20:14-15).

## ⚜ GETTING IN POSITION ⚜

As God is positioning you in your place of authority, you will need to learn how to use His Word.

- How skilled are you with the word of righteousness? How well will you be able to wield the Sword of the Spirit in the day of battle?

Give the Word of God first place in your life. Today, make studying and learning from the meat of God's Word a priority. Because of fatherlessness a whole generation is dying on the battlefield.

- How can the Church better respond to the need for more spiritual fathers?
- What does a spiritual father look like?
- What kind of person do you think God is looking for to step into this position of authority?
- If you are called to be a David in this generation, what can you do to fulfill your part in raising up the next generation?

# CHAPTER 7

# PERFECTED IN LOVE

*Whoever keeps His word, truly the love of*
*God is perfected in him*
(1 John 2:5).

The picture we see of David's heart toward Jonathan represents the Father's heart toward us—one covenanted to love and show kindness forever. As Jonathan and David entered into a covenant that would last for all generations, so God has entered into a covenant with His children. That covenant—God's Word—remains in force for any who by faith keep it. As long as we keep His Word, His Word will keep us. It is the Word of God at work in our hearts that perfects us because it embodies His love—God's love *"poured out in our hearts"* (Rom. 5:5).

When we speak of *perfection* here, we are really talking about "maturity." It is through the perfecting—or maturing—of God's love in us that we become spiritually "of legal age" to operate in God's Kingdom. And it is through obeying God's Word kept in our heart that God's love grows and becomes wisdom in our lives. This process of maturing is what brings us into alignment and positions us for authority. The purpose of the wilderness tests, of becoming skilled in the word of righteousness, of taking our places in the Kingdom as spiritual fathers and heirs, is maturity. Yes, God desires that the Body of Christ *"may grow up in all things into Him who is the head—Christ— from whom the whole body, joined and knit together by what every joint supplies…causes growth of the body for the edifying of itself in love"* (Eph. 4:15-16). That is God's intention for His Church. But in order for you and I to take our places—our positions—of authority that will enable us to walk in power under the sovereign hand of God, we must be matured and perfected in His love.

> *The purpose of the wilderness tests, of becoming skilled in the word of righteousness, of taking our places in the Kingdom as spiritual fathers and heirs, is maturity.*

Promotion in the Kingdom of God requires that you demonstrate a level of spiritual maturity. Until you firmly grasp the foundation and framework of that maturity—the love of God working in and through you—you will never make it to the seat of authority God has prepared for you. In order to get into the alignment necessary to fulfill the assignment God has designated especially for you, you must be perfected in love. It is through exercising that love—through obedience to His love—that you are able to pass every test. His love is your plumb line; it is the essence of who you are becoming; it is what God is calling you to reveal in the earth as His son or daughter. It is how you make Him known. First John 4:12 states, *"No one has seen God at any time,"* but that, *"If we love one another, God abides in us, and His love has been perfected in us."*

> *Promotion in the Kingdom of God requires that you demonstrate a level of spiritual maturity.*

The engine that propels you to your place of authority is fueled by love. It is God's love that empowers you, and the fuel line of that love is God's Word. The love that brings clarity, wisdom, and authority is *"every word that proceeds from the mouth of God"* (Matt. 4:4). That Word is Jesus made manifest *in you*. Without a revelation of that Word—those seeds of God's supernatural, yoke-breaking, bondage-destroying love—you will have no hope of passing the bread test. It is a revelation of that love—of being God's beloved child in whom He is well pleased—that gives you any hope of passing the identity test. And if you are not motivated by that love, and that love alone, you will never pass the authority test. It is a revelation of God's love for you and within you that will get you out of the shadows of any cave, tomb, or prison and on your way to your seat of authority.

## NO FEAR IN LOVE

*There is no fear in love* [dread does not exist], *but full-grown* (complete, perfect) *love turns fear out of doors and expels every trace of terror! For fear brings with it the thought of punishment, and* [so] *he who is afraid has not reached the full maturity of love* [is not yet grown into love's complete perfection] (1 John 4:18 AMP).

The fruit of God's love perfected in you is fearlessness. When you are alone in a dark cave or among wild beasts in the wilderness, you will fear no evil because

God is with you. (See Psalm 23:4.) It is the Word of God spoken over you—His Word of promise—that girds your heart in those desolate places. That Word is meant to take root and mature in you so it empowers you to deal with any fear that opposes you; this is the Word you cultivate and develop when you come out of the wilderness. It is a unique revelation of God's love that He would have you reveal to others. You are the keeper of that distinct Word—that aspect of God's love—that will dispel fear and darkness in the region you are sent to.

Whenever God speaks to you, whenever a Word from God enters your heart, it is His love that is being *"shed abroad"* (Rom. 5:5 KJV) within you. It is a building block of your maturity. God's loving presence fertilizes the soil of your heart so that every Word ever sown into your spirit—every incorruptible seed of His Word—comes to life. That word

> *You are the keeper of that distinct Word—that aspect of God's love—that will dispel fear and darkness in the region you are sent to.*

becomes flesh in you; it bears fruit, the fruit of love, in your life. (See Galatians 5:22.) The Word kept in your heart is the very presence of God—the essence of God, which *is love*, for we know *"God is love, and he who abides in love abides in God, and God in him"* (1 John 4:16). That presence of love brings freedom from fear, for we also know that, *"Where the Spirit of the Lord is, there is liberty"* (2 Cor. 3:17).

When God's living Word comes alive in you, you must cultivate it. Like the keeper of a garden, you must tend to the Word in your heart. Let's go back to First John 2:5 (KJV), *"Whoso keepeth His word, in him verily is the love of God perfected: hereby know we that we are in Him."* What word are you supposed to keep? The one He spoke to you. How do you keep that word? You keep it by committing to live by it; that is how you set in motion the principle of living by *"every word that proceeds from the mouth of God."* We have already learned that this is the first step to getting out of the wilderness. You say to yourself, "I will keep the word. I will cultivate it. I will meditate on it day and night." We get a glimpse of what this means by looking at the Lord's instructions to the children of Israel in Deuteronomy 11:18-19:

> *You shall lay up these words of mine in your heart and in your soul, and bind them as a sign on your hand, and they shall be as frontlets between your eyes. You shall teach them to your children, speaking of them when you sit in your house, when*

*you walk by the way, when you lie down,*
*and when you rise up.*

When you keep the Word, meditate on the Word, speak the Word, and pray the Word that He has spoken to you, you are cultivating the Word in your life and causing the love of God to mature in you. The more God's love grows and matures in your heart, the less fear will be able to deceive you, trip you up, and hold you back. You may not understand it with your intellect, but the peace of God begins to stand guard over your mind; your hope in God begins to anchor your soul, and you begin to partake of God's divine nature making *"your call and election sure, for if you do these things you will never stumble"* (2 Pet. 1:10).

Every temptation is based in fear. Every failed character test is a result of fear. You don't live by every word that proceeds from the mouth of God because you are afraid. Out of fear you clamor to take hold of what you can see rather than fully embracing the substance of things hoped for—the evidence of things *unseen*. You are afraid of rejection or betrayal so you don't fully embrace your identity in Christ. Afraid of failure, you ultimately fail every authority test because you don't trust God enough to submit yourself to Him and others. You attempt to promote yourself rather than humble yourself before God and the people He places in authority over you.

Your only hope of overcoming your every fear is to allow the love of God to be perfected—or fully matured—in your heart. A key to doing that is abiding in His presence. Listen to the words Jesus spoke in John 15:4-5: *"As the branch cannot bear fruit of itself, unless it abides in the vine, neither can you, unless you abide in Me. I am the vine, you are the branches. He who abides in Me, and I in him, bears much fruit; for without Me you can do nothing."* Abide in the vine, abide in His presence, abide in the Holy Spirit, and let the presence of God continually cook the Word that is in you. The Word of God in your heart is like bread in the oven; allow God's presence to turn up the heat in your heart.

In First John 4:17-18 (NLT) we read, "As we live in God, our love grows more perfect." Then we are told the reason: "So we will not be afraid on the day of judgment, but we can face Him with confidence because we live like Jesus here in this world." We are reminded that, "Such love has no fear, because perfect love expels all fear." And finally John concludes that, "If we are afraid, it is for fear of punishment, and this shows that we have not fully experienced His perfect love," or as the Amplified Bible says, we have "not reached the full maturity of love."

There it is. You have to let the love of God reach full maturity. Wherever the Word of God is growing in your life, there the love of God is maturing. And wherever God's love is perfected in you, there you will have boldness and confidence in the Day of Judgment. You will be tested whether you are living by faith, whether you are confident of your identity, and whether you are submitted to God's authority. And because God's love has reached full maturity in you, you will pass every test because every fear has been quenched. That's the power of love—the love of the Father working in and revealed through you.

## THE FATHER'S LOVE REVEALED

*That which we have seen and heard we declare to you, that you also may have fellowship with us; and truly our fellowship is with the Father and with His Son Jesus Christ. And these things we write to you that your joy may be full* (1 John 1:3-4).

You and I are an expression of a Word that proceeded from the Father—namely Jesus—by whom all things were created, seen and unseen. We read that the Word brought life and was the light of men. Your life comes from this living Word—this living Bread. As you partake of this Bread, you enter into covenant with God the Father and become one flesh with Christ. He is calling you to become one with Him—to abide in Him, and He in you. (See John 15:4-5.) That is why there is *"no condemnation to those who are in Christ Jesus, who do not walk according to the flesh, but according to the Spirit"* (Rom. 8:1). This is why God makes statements such as, *"I, even I, am He who blots out your transgressions for My own sake"* (Isa. 43:25). God has redeemed you for His own sake. Why? Because He loves you as much as He loves Jesus.

He already knew you before you were formed in your mother's womb. He had already pre-designed you and pre-engineered a plan for your life before you were ever conceived. You are no surprise to Him. From the beginning He loved you so deeply that He set into motion everything you would need for victory before the foundation of the world. He had already imagined, designed, and planned your entire existence.

But why bother with this earthly existence in the first place? Why not skip ahead to the good things God has in store for you in eternity? If this life is but a stepping-stone to Heaven, why not take a zip-line straight into the Father's arms? Wouldn't that be more loving?

God is as interested in developing your love for Him as He is in revealing His love for you. It is through your expanding revelation of that love that you learn to increasingly love Him. He is stretching your capacity to receive and give love. God's love for you is so great that He went through all He did so He could have a relationship with you and so enjoy experiencing your ever deepening love for Him—even as you are filled with all the fullness of His love for you. (See Ephesians 3:18-20.) His pleasure is to raise you up and teach you, mold you, and perfect you in His love.

He predestined this earthly life for you so that you could learn His ways—so that you could learn to love and trust Him and walk in faith as a result of your own choice. God wants to show you how to live by every word that proceeds from His mouth. He is teaching you day by day to live as one with Him through Christ. You are being changed from glory to glory through His Word at work in your heart.

Jesus said, *"The words that I speak to you are spirit, and they are life"* (John 6:63). He then says He cleanses and sanctifies you by the washing of water by the Word. We read in Ephesians 5:25-30 that Christ so loved the Church that He, *"gave Himself for her, that He might sanctify and cleanse her with the washing of water by the word."* He does this so that, *"He might present her to Himself...not having spot or wrinkle or any such thing, but that she should be holy and without blemish."* This is a sacred love that Paul likens to the deep, abiding love of marriage. He instructs husbands *"to love their wives as their own bodies,"* because in a covenant of marriage, *"he who loves his wife loves himself."* And that's how Christ loves you: *"For we are members of His body, of His flesh and of His bones."* Christ loves you as His own body.

Just as Jesus and the Father are one, so Christ and the Church are one. Just as Jesus was able to declare, *"He who has seen Me has seen the Father"* (John 14:9), so should a Christian be able to say, "If you have seen me, you have seen Jesus." But until, as Jesus did, you are able to walk with God as your own heavenly Father, you will not be fully established in your own identity as His beloved child. You will not be able to reveal Jesus the Son or God the Father—and that is your central purpose.

Your purpose, therefore, is intimately tied to your identity. Jesus did but one thing: reveal the Father. The Father did but one thing: reveal His Son. You are to do but one thing: reveal the Father through the Son by how you love others. God helps you do that by first and foremost establishing your identity in Christ. Through the Word you are able to renew your mind regarding whose it is God has created you to be: His cherished child, adopted heir, righteous, worthy, and loved. You are not an accident, mishap, imposter, or unwanted.

When I came to Christ—repatriated from the kingdom of darkness into the Kingdom of Light—the first thing God did was give me a new identity. He gave me a new passport and established a new identity within me before He began to reveal His purpose for me. He helped me to understand that any gift or impartation would never be as important as my identity in Him. The Father would whisper in my ear and say, "You're unique. You're an original. I love you just the way you are, and although I have wired you for a special purpose, the most

> *It would never matter who I was to other people, but it would always matter who He was to me.*

important thing to remember is whose you are. You are My beloved son in whom I am well pleased."

God told me, "It doesn't matter what you do for Me—what matters is who I am to you."

It would never matter who I was to other people, but it would always matter who He was to me. While He began to confirm His love for me and reveal Himself to me, He would say, "Do you know why you call Me *Father*? Do you know why you have this grace and this peace in the midst of the most awkward circumstances: while you live in a car, while nobody believes you are called to do a thing? Do you know why I can call you My son?" God would always remind me that I had this wonderful relationship with Him because of His Son, Jesus.

The love that I received from the Father caused me to turn to Jesus and say, "Thank You, Jesus. Thank You for not being too insecure to share Your own Father with me. Thank You for dying on the cross so You could make Him available to me—so that I could be adopted by Him. Thank You for coming in human form so that You could reveal Your Father to me." Now I have a Father; now I have an identity. Now I know whose I am because I know to whom I belong. I can say to Him, "You are the substance of which I am formed; You and I share the same DNA because You gave me Your Spirit—the same Spirit that proceeds from the Father—as a seal of the covenant You have made with me. The Holy Spirit is the seal of my sonship."

> *You see, obedience is a response to a work that God has done in you—not a means to attaining something.*

You see, obedience is a response to a work that God has done in you—not a means to attaining something. That was the law. Obedience without grace is mere religion, and grace without obedience is lasciviousness. But as sons and heirs, we are obedient because we love the Father and He loves us. Love obeys. Christ was obedient unto death. Jesus put it this way, *"When you obey My* commandments, you remain in My love, just as I obey My Father's commandments and remain in His love" (John 15:10 NLT).

In John 14:22 we read where Judas asks the Lord, *"How is it that You will manifest Yourself to us, and not to the world?"* Jesus gives this telling response:

> *If anyone loves Me, he will keep My word; and My Father will love him, and We will come to him and make Our home with him. He who does not love Me does not keep My words; and the word which you hear is not Mine but the Father's who sent Me* (John 14:23-24).

God reveals Himself to those who obey Him.

## A REVELATION OF THE FATHER

> *If you had known Me, you would have known My Father also; and from now on you know Him and have seen Him* (John 14:7).

What I have come to experience over the many years I have been in ministry—especially in regards to those who are in positions of leadership—is that a revelation of the Father is an essential key to achieving the thing God has called you to do.

We talked a little bit about identity. We talked about how your identity stems from your relationship with the Father. Your identity is not defined by who you are on any given day; it is about to whom you belong. Take your last name. Your last name tells you who you are of, where you came from, or to whom you belong. Your identity is tied up in your name. It's the same when you become a Christian. When you come to know God as your Father—when you accept Christ as your Savior—you take on that name and experience life through the filter of that relationship. Your identity is defined by your relationship with your Father.

> *Your identity is not defined by who you are on any given day; it is about to whom you belong.*

Identifying with God the Father—engaging in that love relationship—redefines you. It is at the core of all you are now or will ever be. Unlike an earthly father who may only tolerate your differences, your heavenly Father celebrates your differences. He celebrates what's different about you because He has wired you for a unique purpose—for a unique function in the earth to bring Him glory in a way only His creativity expressed through you can. You are a distinct expression of the Father in Christ. This is where your strength and your life come from.

In John 14:8 (NLT), when Philip asks Jesus, "Lord, show us the Father, and we will be satisfied." Jesus is taken aback. He replies, "Have I been with you all this time, Philip, and yet you still don't know who I am? Anyone who has seen Me has seen the Father! So why are you asking Me to show Him to you?" (John 14:9 NLT). Philip's question represents a hunger to know the meaning of "fatherhood."

Today, more than ever, we are living in a generation that does not know what a true father looks like. We have many instructors, but not many fathers. While instructors inform, fathers impart. Fathers don't replicate themselves; they produce original expressions of Christ.

> *While instructors inform, fathers impart.*

Authentic fatherhood is at the center of what God is doing. As God is maturing His people and preparing them to walk in princely authority, He is positioning spiritual fathers throughout the Church. God is stirring His Davids to raise up a generation of leaders with the nurture and admonition of the Lord. Are you that David?

In Matthew 11:27, Jesus tells us, "All things have been delivered to Me by My Father, and no one knows the Son except the Father. Nor does anyone know the Father except the Son, and the one to whom the Son wills to reveal Him." How does the Father reveal the Son? He reveals Him by the Spirit. Doesn't the Word of God say you cannot come to the Son except the Father draw you first? How does Jesus reveal the Father? He does it by the Spirit of God. Matthew 10:20 says when you are asked to give an answer for the hope that is in you, take no thought what you must say, "For it is not you who will be speaking—it will be the Spirit of your Father speaking through you."

In Matthew 10:20 we see the Spirit of the Father that reveals the Son, but in Galatians 4:6 we see the Spirit of the Son that reveals the Father: *"God has sent the Spirit of His Son into our hearts, prompting us to call out, 'Abba, Father.'"* It is the same Spirit—the Spirit of God—that compels you to cry out to God as a child cries out for his or her earthly father. God's Spirit reveals to your spirit that He is the Father and that you are His beloved son or daughter.

When the Father speaks regarding His Son, Jesus, He approves, honors, and affirms Him because He is His Father. When the Father speaks from Heaven regarding you, He approves, affirms, and reveals that you are His beloved child. Your spirit bears witness with His Spirit. He is affirming His Fatherhood and your adoption into the family of God. God dotes on you as much as He does Jesus. He loves you with the same love and delights in bearing witness to your adoption as much as He does in revealing His only begotten Son. A revelation of the Father's love for you will bring comfort to your orphaned soul. A revelation of the Father will bring rest.

## ENTERING THE FATHER'S REST

*Come to Me, all you who labor and are heavy laden, and I will give you rest. Take My yoke upon you and learn from Me, for I am gentle and lowly in heart, and you will find rest for your souls. For My yoke is easy and My burden is light* (Matthew 11:28-30).

Some of you who have stepped out into what God is calling you to do feel as though you have labored a bit. You have been through some situations, had to believe God through some hardships, and have probably suffered in some of your relationships. It may seem the enemy is busy working against you on every level. A crisis hits and you find yourself saying, "Lord, what do I do?" Sometimes you feel you've blown it. How can you ask God for help when you've made a mistake, misjudged, or just made some bad choices? There are times you find yourself completely broken, not knowing what to do.

And then Jesus says to you, "Come to Me, all you who labor and are heavy laden, and I will give you rest." Now listen to the statement Jesus makes next, which seems a contradiction. He says, "Take My yoke upon you and learn of Me, for I am gentle and lowly in heart, and you will find rest for your souls." That seems well enough, but then He makes this next statement: "For My yoke is easy and My burden is light." Why is He saying His yoke is easy and His burden is light when He has to bear all the sin of the world? We know in the Garden of Gethsemane He was sweating blood. We know the anxiety of His soul when He fell on His face before the Father and prayed, "O My Father, if it is possible, let this cup pass from Me; nevertheless, not as I will, but as You will" (Matt. 26:39).

In the midst of all that Jesus was going through, He tells His disciples, *"My yoke is easy and my burden is light."* How could He make that statement? What did Jesus really mean when He spoke those words? The verse just prior to that gives a clue; Jesus said, *"Come to Me...I will give you rest."* What is this "rest" that Jesus gives? It is the rest of a revelation of the Father. Your revelation of the Father must exceed your revelation of the circumstances that weigh upon you. Jesus is saying, "My yoke is easy because the revelation of My Father is greater than My yoke—greater than the burden." Yes, Jesus had a yoke; He had a burden to go to the cross on behalf of humanity. But He had something else—something much greater.

In John 17:26 (NIV), He said to the Father, "I have made You known to them, and will continue to make You known in order that the love You have for Me may be in them and that I Myself may be in them." Jesus was motivated by the love the Father had for Him. There was something about the love He experienced with the Father that compelled Him to lay down His life. You see that love relationship and intimate fellowship with the Father

> *Your revelation of the Father must exceed your revelation of the circumstances that weigh upon you.*

should be at the core of all you do. Jesus is saying, "If I see My Father do it, I do it; if I hear My Father say it, that is what I will say." Jesus was a living demonstration of the Father, "The works you see Me doing, it is My Father in Me doing these works." Jesus' character and identity were inseparable from the Father's.

Romans 8:37 states, *"Yet in all these things we are more than conquerors through Him who loved us."* The measure with which you know His love is the measure with which you conquer in life. Being defined as *"more than conquerors"* speaks of identity. Conquering is not an event; it's not a battle you go through and win. It is a state of being. Because you know the love He loves you with in the midst of your situation—because you have a revelation of that love—you begin to conquer in any situation in your life. Grace will get you through a problem, faith will give you the victory, but love will make you *more than a conqueror.*

Leaders, don't forget the love with which He loves you while you lay down your life for His cause. Because at the end of the day it is who you become and who you are that is going to carry you through the opposition that you face. The enemy knows when you know who you are. He doesn't like messing with God's children, because when a son or daughter manifests, they destroy the works of the devil; they manifest the glory of their Father. They manifest something that comes directly from the Father that the devil can't come against. That is what a revelation of the Father in your heart does in the spirit realm.

Everything Jesus did was a result of His revelation of the Father. In John 6:57 He says, *"The living Father sent Me, and I live because of the Father."* If Jesus could not live apart from the Father, how can you? After all the beatings and scourging—after all Jesus endured even before He was nailed to the cross—and then the hours of agony as He hung on the cross—it was only after He was abandoned by God that He cried out, *"My God, My God, why have You forsaken Me?'...and breathed His last"* (Mark 15:34).

Jesus did not know how to live apart from the Father. When God forsook Him, that was it. He could take anything except being apart from His Father. He said in John 6:57, *"As the living Father sent Me...I live because of the Father."* It wasn't the nails that killed Jesus; it wasn't the stripes on His back nor the crown of thorns on His head that killed Him; it was separation from the Father. But why did the Father forsake Jesus? So He could say to you and I, *"I'll never leave you nor forsake you."* Jesus wore a crown of thorns so you and I could wear a crown of glory—so we could be called sons and daughters of God.

You will experience obstacles, trials, tests, and situations in your life, but if you have a revelation of the Father, you will make it through every one with your crown intact. What is the purpose of you accomplishing much for God if in the end you don't recognize yourself when you look in the mirror? Isn't it better to live in the assurance of who you are and to rest in the knowledge of whose you are? I promise you, if you take hold of who you really are as an heir *with* Christ—fully embracing your spiritual lineage—the fruit will show forth in your life and you will accomplish so much more. At the same time, what you accomplish should never define you; all you achieve should point to the Father.

## SHOWING FORTH GOD'S POWER AND GLORY

> *O God, do not forsake me, until I declare Your strength to this generation, Your power to everyone who is to come* (Psalm 71:18).

There are too few spiritual fathers in this day and era. As God convicted me of this, He showed me Psalm 71:18, and here is what I heard Him say, "There's a prophetic cry of a man with silver hair. He is crying out to God, 'Oh Lord, when I'm old and gray-haired forsake me not, until I've shown Your power and Your glory to my generation and the generation that is yet to come.'" I began to see that the heart of the Father has always been to raise up a remnant in every generation, and if that remnant is successful, it will take God's message—God's intention—to the rest of that generation. If that generation is successful, it will touch the generation that is yet to come.

Yet I noticed a gap between the generations—something causing a breakdown and keeping God's power and glory from showing forth. That gap is fatherlessness. As leaders, we need to learn to impact the next generation with the spirit of fatherhood.

I am ashamed to say that my generation is fatherless. We have homosexuality because of fatherlessness. We have sexual immorality because of fatherlessness. We have drug and alcohol abuse because of fatherlessness. When you find out who you are—to whom you belong—when you get a revelation of your identity—you won't need to do drugs. Every problem in the Bible comes from not knowing the Father. We need to leave a legacy of fatherhood for the next generation so they can be equipped to do the right thing. They need to get a revelation of who their heavenly Father is and that He will show up for them in the midst of any crisis. They need spiritual fathers to disciple them and point them to the Father just as Jesus did in His earthly ministry.

*I promise you, if you take hold of who you really are as an heir with Christ—fully embracing your spiritual lineage—the fruit will show forth in your life and you will accomplish so much more.*

Isaiah 53:10 tells us it pleased the Father to bruise His Son. Why would it please the Father to bruise His Son?

John 17:23 gives the answer: *"that they may be made perfect in one, and that the world may know that You have sent Me, and have loved them as You have loved Me."* When God the Father saw His Son bruised, He saw you and I healed. He saw you and I coming to fellowship and relationship with Him. That's why we are told in Isaiah 43:25 that He *"blots out your transgressions for* [His] *own sake."* We think He did it for us, but He did it for His own sake. That's the nature of our God; He loves us so much that He can't stand being separated from us.

God chastises and disciplines you because He loves you. He wants you to be perfect. He wants you to grow up strong and healthy physically, mentally, and spiritually. He wants to show forth His power and glory through you. I look forward to the Father's rebukes because that tells me He loves me. I look forward to His correction because it tells me He is present and paying attention; I can locate Him in every situation or circumstance. When the Father begins to bring correction—to bring alignment—it is a sign that He is drawing close to me. That is edifying.

This is what God is calling you to do with those He brings for you to father: to be present with them, draw them close, show them you are paying attention, and offer correction when it is needed, because you love them as a father loves a child. Just as the Father wants to bring alignment into your life so that you can be positioned for authority, so should you be bringing alignment into the lives of those of the next generation. As a spiritual parent, you can help prepare those coming after you to take their seats of authority. In fact, passing on a revelation of authority will involve passing on a revelation of fatherhood. If we are to eliminate fatherlessness in future generations, we will have to raise our spiritual sons to one day be fathers; we will have to teach and train those coming after how to leave a legacy of fatherhood in the next generation.

That's what it's all about. That's what being a spiritual leader is all about—being a father by revealing the Father and training up future fathers by sharing a revelation of the Father. If that's who we become, then we will have become an expression of His leadership on the earth; we will have succeeded at demonstrating and expressing the Father. This is how we show forth God's power and glory.

When you live by a revelation of the Father, and live to reveal Him to others, you become who you were destined to be. You will pass every test because you know to whom you belong. You will take your seat of authority because of who you are revealing. Let this prayer be your heart's cry as you take your place of authority in the Kingdom: *"O God, do not forsake me, until I declare Your strength to this generation, Your power to everyone who is to come"* (Ps. 71:18).

## YOUR TIME HAS COME

*"Before I formed you in the womb I knew you; before you were born I sanctified you; I ordained you a prophet to the nations." Then said I: "Ah, Lord God! Behold, I cannot speak, for I am a youth." But the Lord said to me: "Do not say, 'I am a youth,' for you shall go to all to whom I send you, and whatever I command you, you shall speak"* (Jeremiah 1:5-7).

As Davids are being called out and raised up to take their positions as fathers in the Body of Christ, so God is calling out to Jonathans to take their places as sons. Just as God knew David and Jonathan before He formed them, and ordained them before they were born into positions of authority, so has God ordained you for a specific purpose. You were set apart for your position of authority before the foundation of the earth. God planned, formed, and wired you for the thing you are called to before you were even born.

Now you find yourself in a season when all of your life experiences are coming together to bring you to the place God has destined for you—a place that exceeds your current understanding. You find yourself responding to God,

"How can it be me?" I believe God is challenging you to do certain things far greater than you thought possible. The Lord is saying to you, *"Don't say, 'I'm too young,' for you must go wherever I send you and say whatever I tell you"* (Jer. 1:7 NLT).

There is a specific jurisdiction—a particular people— you are called to, and a special message you have been given to speak. It will take courage, but God says He will be with you every step of the way. *"Don't be afraid of the people, for I will be with you and will protect you. I, the Lord, have spoken!"* (Jer. 1:8). The Lord has promised to equip and empower you. He will anoint you just as He did Jeremiah. *"Then the Lord put forth His hand and touched my mouth, and the Lord said to me: 'Behold, I have put My words in your mouth'"* (Jer. 1:9).

> *If we could get a revelation of what the Word of God in our mouth can do, combined with His love shed abroad in our hearts, life on earth would be more like it is in Heaven.*

That is exciting to think about. But too often we stop here—or worse, we take the power of God's Word in our mouth for granted. If we could get a revelation of what the Word of God in our mouth can do, combined with His love shed abroad in our hearts, life on earth would be more like it is in Heaven. We could make a significant difference in the lives of the people God sends us to.

This is what we find at the heart of God's will concerning Jeremiah: "See, I have this day set you over the nations and over the kingdoms, to root out and to pull down, to destroy and to throw down, to build and to plant" (Jer. 1:10). God was giving him authority; He was calling Jeremiah to take his seat of authority in order to radically transform the regions He was sending him to. God gave Jeremiah a revelation of his call, because his season to speak with power and authority had come.

As your season approaches, you will begin to get a revelation of God's power at work in you. God will bring forth new and fresh revelation concerning the secret things you are carrying on His behalf. This is the season the Church is entering. God is revealing to believers everywhere what the Body of Christ has long been harboring on His behalf. He is preparing men and women to take their seats of authority so they will be in a position to fulfill what He has called them to do from the beginning. Be open to how God is moving you because He is preparing and positioning you—His Church—for an entirely new level of authority on the earth: *To set you over the nations and over the kingdoms, to root out and to pull down, to destroy and to throw down, to build and to plant*" (Jer. 1:10).

It is time to come out of the wilderness. It is time to

come out of the shadows. David was not meant to stay in the cave, nor Joseph in prison, nor Daniel in the lion's den. God called them out and raised them up. You may feel like your dream is already dead and buried, or you have simply gotten comfortable with being asleep in your tomb, but just as Jesus called Lazarus forth, He is calling you. Just as God raised Jesus up, He will raise you up; He will breathe new life into you, your situation, or your dreams. There is no tomb, or cave, or dungeon so deep and dark that the light of Christ can't reach it. *"For it is the God who commanded light to shine out of darkness, who has shone in our hearts to give the light of the knowledge of the glory of God in the face of Jesus Christ"* (2 Cor. 4:6).

The Word of the Lord is saying: "Awake, you who sleep. Arise from the dead, and Christ will give you light." Arise! Your time has come. You are positioned for authority. Step up to the platform and sit down in the seat of authority God has prepared for you.

> *Then He closed the book, and gave it back*
> *to the attendant and sat down* (Luke 4:20).

 **GETTING IN POSITION**

Identifying with God the Father—engaging in that

love relationship—redefines you. It is at the core of all you are now or will ever be.

- How has your relationship with the Father redefined you?
- Who do you hope to become as a result of that relationship?

In order for you take your seat, or fulfill your place of authority under the sovereign hand of God, you must be matured and perfected in His love.

- How does exercising—or obeying— God's love enable you to pass every test?
- How does God's Word in your heart empower you to overcome the fear that is at the root of every temptation?

What God reveals to you through His Word is what He would have you reveal to others. The distinctive aspect of God's love will dispel fear and darkness in the region you are sent to.

- What is the Word you have been cultivating in your heart—the Word you hold onto that strengthens and restores you?

- What aspect of God's love have you been entrusted with?

Pray that God will show you what part of Him He wants you to reveal to others.

When you live by a revelation of the Father, and live to reveal Him to others, you become who you are destined to be. You will pass every test because you know to Whom you belong. You will take your seat of authority because of Who you are revealing.

Let this prayer be your heart's cry as you take your place of authority in the Kingdom: *"O God, do not forsake me, until I declare Your strength to this generation, Your power to everyone who is to come"* (Psalm 71:18).

Be open to how God is moving you because He is preparing and positioning you for an entirely new level of authority on the earth.

# CONCLUDING THOUGHTS

The secret to fulfilling your divine assignment is getting into your God-ordained position of authority. Understanding your authority in Christ, taking your seat of authority in the Kingdom, and leaving a legacy of authority by empowering a generation of leaders to step into their unique places of authority are what fulfilling your divine assignment is all about. You must know how to position yourself to operate in the supernatural authority you will need to fulfill your divine assignment.

In Chapter 1 you learned about the significance of authority—why your seat of authority is so important. In Chapter 2 you learned about the history of the seat—how God ordered authority in the heavens and how lucifer, who held the highest place of authority among the angels, coveted the only seat higher than his: God's very throne. Lucifer lost his seat of authority in seeking God's seat and fell to earth. When God created Adam, He gave him the highest seat of authority on the earth, which he lost by believing lucifer—and so man fell. Jesus, the Son of God, came to earth fashioned as a man to retake that earthly seat in order to fulfill His divine assignment. He succeeded in fulfilling His eternal purpose on the cross, triumphing over satan and stripping him of all authority and power. Jesus then ascended to the right hand of God to sit far above all principalities and powers; He positioned redeemed man with Him there far above satan and his demons.

*You must know how to position yourself to operate in the supernatural authority you will need to fulfill your divine assignment.*

We continue to bruise satan's head under our feet as we operate and function in the seat of authority God has for us. The implication is twofold: First is your personal authority in your own sphere of influence; second is the corporate authority you have to function in your divine assignment on earth.

When you operate from this place of authority, you are positioned for divine favor and blessing. When you position yourself under the hand of God, you are protected, anointed, and blessed. The extent to which you succeed in fulfilling your assignment depends on how you position yourself under the sovereign hand of God. You position yourself in this place of power by aligning your life with the will and Word of God. Authority is a result of alignment, which must precede the fulfillment of your assignment. The process of walking in alignment is what I call the *Plumb Line Principle.* When you understand the significance of aligning your every thought, word, and action with God's Word, you will be in a position to pass the wilderness tests introduced in Chapter 5. When you successfully pass the bread test, identity test, and authority test, you will pass from your desert, cave, or prison to the Promised Land made available from your divine place of authority.

> *Taking your seat of authority is about becoming a leader who has mastered the art of authoritative love.*

God tests you to know if you can be trusted with authority. He tests whether you will submit to the authority of His Word. He is teaching you about your authority as His child, and the necessity of submitting to the authority of others. In Chapter 6 you learned how Saul was neither able to submit to God's authority nor honor the authority God placed in those around him—including Jonathan and David. Saul relied on his own strength and his own sword by which he ultimately died. We see how

Jonathan failed the identity test because he never fully understood his own potential or who he was as a son and an heir. While Saul abused his authority and Jonathan didn't understand his authority, David submitted to God's authority and demonstrated how to walk in the power of godly, kingdom authority. David shows us how to pass every wilderness test—but most importantly, the authority test.

In Chapter 7 you learned the importance of maturing in your authority by allowing God's love to grow and be perfected in you. You learned the eternal significance of using your authority to reveal God's love and how God's love governs and empowers your authority as a believer. Being perfected in love is at the core of fulfilling your divine assignment; it is the key to growing up and walking in true authority through which you reveal the Father. The central, eternal purpose of every divine assignment is to reveal the Father.

Taking your seat of authority is about becoming a leader who has mastered the art of authoritative love. You read about the leadership attributes of David, the lessons of managing his God-given authority and navigating the traps and pitfalls that came with it; how he was tested time and again and completely submitted to God and those whom God placed in authority over him. It was through those tests and triumphs that God trained him to use his seat of authority to advance the Kingdom and bring glory to God.

God is training up a generation of Davids to take their seats of authority. He is positioning His Church to walk in a level of authority she has yet to embrace. This is a season of alignment. When every member of the Body of Christ aligns his or her heart with the heart of God, there will be a divine synergy. You will feel a new energy and unity flowing through your church and community. You will begin to increasingly operate from a sacred, powerful place of authority—protected, empowered, and positioned to fulfill your divine assignment on the earth.

The purpose of this book is to help you move out of the shadows into the light. My desire is that you no longer remain in the wilderness and be divinely positioned under the sovereign hand of God unleashing your hidden potential. May you conquer your giants and give birth to the promises of God. May you grasp God's eternal perspective of your life on earth and dare to live a life of eternal significance leaving a legacy to generations to come.

## MINISTRY INFORMATION

Covenant of Life Ministries
Covenant of Life Media Inc.
PO Box 27055
Lethbridge, AB T1K 6Z8, Canada
**E-mail: info@covenantoflife.org**
**Website: www.covenantoflife.org**
Phone: 1-877-220-3030
Outside North America, Phone: 403-329-3038

## MINISTRY RESOURCES

**THE PLUMB LINE** *(Available on CD & DVD)*

This product addresses various questions that we ask ourselves:

* What is the Plumb Line?
* How can I align myself to Heaven's Plumb Line?
* Is there a larger reason for why my prayers are unanswered?
* Is my life built accordingly to the Plumb Line?

**GOD: PHARAOH OR FATHER?** *(Available on CD & DVD)*

How do you see God? Do you see Him as a loving Father or a Taskmaster?

In addition to understanding God's true nature, this dynamic message of hope will also help you discern your identity, passion, and purpose.

**LIFESTYLE EVANGELISM** *(6 disc CD & DVD SET)*

In this powerful training school you will learn:

* How to share your faith.
* How to reach out to people with a different belief system.
* Much from special question and answer sessions.

Additional copies of this book and other
book titles from DESTINY IMAGE are
available at your local bookstore.

Call toll-free: 1-800-722-6774.

Send a request for a catalog to:

**Destiny Image® Publishers, Inc.**
P.O. Box 310
Shippensburg, PA 17257-0310

*"Speaking to the Purposes of God for this
Generation and for the Generations to Come."*

**For a complete list of our titles,
visit us at www.destinyimage.com.**